Maps, Charts, Graphs - Transparencies
TEACHING SUGGESTIONS

Color Transparency 1 ■ page 3
Skill: Finding directions

■ Before displaying CT 1, write the terms *cardinal directions* and *intermediate directions* on the chalkboard and review them briefly. Tell students that north is one of the cardinal directions. What are the others? Determine which classroom wall faces north. Have students identify the south, east, and west walls of the classroom. Then have students locate the northeast, northwest, southeast, and southwest corners of the classroom. Ask students how information about directions is shown on a map. Review the term *compass rose*.

Display **CT 1**. Have a volunteer circle the direction line and mark the intermediate directions on it. Have students name the country that is north of the United States (Canada) and the states that are west of North Carolina (Tennessee), south of Oklahoma (Texas), northwest of Idaho (Washington), and northeast of Iowa (Wisconsin). What state would students be in if they traveled one state east from Kansas, then northeast, then north? (Wisconsin) Divide the class into groups to play a game of "Find That State." This game is played by using cardinal and intermediate directions to identify the states shown on CT 1. Each group should choose five states and write two clues about the location of each state using cardinal and intermediate directions. You may wish to provide the following example:

    Clue 1: This state is southwest of Missouri.
    Clue 2: This state is three states south of South Dakota.
    What state is this? (Oklahoma)

Groups can compete to identify states based on each clue. If the state is identified after the first clue, award 5 points to the group. If two clues are necessary, give 3 points. Write each state on the chalkboard and have the class determine which states are missing.

Color Transparency 1 ■ Transmaster 9

■ Divide the class into groups. Each group will need a copy of Transmaster 9, a political map of Africa, and three note cards. Have students draw a compass rose or north arrow on their map and label all the African countries, using the reference map as a guide. The countries of southwest Asia do not need to be labeled. Next have students color the following countries: South Africa, Tanzania, Niger, Senegal, Libya, Ethiopia, Zimbabwe, and Angola. When students have completed these steps, ask each group to write three sets of directions from the first place listed to the other country or countries in each item. Students should use cardinal and intermediate directions in writing their instructions.

    1. from South Africa to Tanzania
    2. from Niger to Senegal to Libya
    3. from Ethiopia to Zimbabwe to Angola

For example, a set of directions for going from Egypt to Nigeria might be as follows: Go south through Sudan, then west through Chad, then southwest to Nigeria. Students may exchange directions and trace each route on their map. Groups should correct any errors and discuss the hazards of bad directions.

Color Transparency 2 ■ page 5
Skill: Using map scale

■ Display **CT 2**. Ask what continent is shown on this map. (Asia) Locate this area on a wall map of the world. What parts of Asia are shown? (eastern and southern) Point to Kabul, Afghanistan. Tell students to imagine that they are taking a trip by van from Kabul to New Delhi, India. How can they tell the distance from Kabul to New Delhi? (by using the map scale) Remind students that *scale* is the relationship between distance on a map and a larger real distance on Earth that it represents. Elicit from students that each inch on a map stands for a certain number of feet or miles on Earth's surface. Most maps provide a *scale bar* to show the relationship between the distances shown on the map and the distances in the real world. How many measured miles are shown on the scale on CT 2? (500) How many kilometers? (800) Judging by this scale, which is a larger unit of measurement—a mile or a kilometer? (mile) Point to the unlabeled mark between 0 and 100 miles on the scale bar. How many miles does this mark represent? (50) What does the mark between 100 and 200 miles represent? (150 miles) between 0 and 200 kilometers? (100 kilometers) Circle Kabul and New Delhi on the map and ask a volunteer to find the distance between these two cities. (about 650 miles or

1100 kilometers —Xian or Shanghai? (Xian ... ...eers can also find the dis...

    1. Colombo, ...0 miles)
    2. Ulan Bato... ...nd Beijing, China (about 750 miles)
    3. Dacca, Bangladesh and Katmandu, Nepal (about 425 miles)

Color Transparency 2 ■ Transmaster 1

■ For this activity, divide the class into pairs. Each pair will need a ruler and a copy of Transmaster 1. Have students add the following scale to their transmasters: $1'' = 310$ miles. Ask students to label the state capitals of California, Idaho, Montana, North Dakota, Minnesota, Wisconsin, Indiana, Kentucky, Arkansas, Texas, New Mexico, and Arizona. Then have students draw lines connecting each of the following cities below and compute the mileage between these cities using the bar scale:

    1. Sacramento, CA to Boise, ID (about 465 miles)
    2. Boise, ID to Helena, MT (about 275 miles)
    3. Helena, MT to St. Paul, MN (about 895 miles)
    4. St. Paul, MN to Madison, WI to Indianapolis, IN (about 510 miles)
    5. Indianapolis, IN to Frankfort, KY (about 155 miles)
    6. Frankfort, KY to Little Rock, AR (about 465 miles)
    7. Little Rock, AR to Austin, TX (about 465 miles)
    8. Austin, TX to Santa Fe, NM (about 585 miles)
    9. Santa Fe, NM to Phoenix, AZ (about 350 miles)
    10. Phoenix, AZ to Sacramento, CA (about 620 miles)

Students can compare distances and rank the trips in order from shortest to longest.

Color Transparency 3 ■ page 6
Skill: Comparing scale

■ Display **CT 3**, covering the map scale on each map. Tell students that the map on the left shows the European country of San Marino. This tiny nation, only 24 square miles in area, is completely surrounded by Italy. Have students name the country shown in the map on the right. (U.S.S.R.) With over 8 million square miles, the U.S.S.R. is the largest country in the world covering parts of both Asia and Europe. Which map shows the larger land area? (map of U.S.S.R.) Ask students on which map they think 1 inch would equal a larger number of miles. (U.S.S.R.) Have students give reasons for their opinions. Uncover the scale bars and have students confirm the accuracy of their answers. Ask students how many measured miles are shown on the map scale for San Marino? (3 miles) for the U.S.S.R.? (1000 miles) Examine the relationship between land area and map scale. Point out that in general the larger the area shown on a map, the smaller the scale is likely to be. ($1'' = 1000$ miles instead of $1'' = 300$ miles) The smaller the area shown, the larger the scale. ($1'' = 3$ miles instead of $1'' = 250$ miles) The larger the scale, the greater the amount of detail that can be shown on a map. Have students take turns finding distances between the following cities:

    1. San Marino: Acquaviva to Faetano (about 4.5 miles)
    2. San Marino: Borgo Maggiore to Fiorentino (about 2 miles)
    3. U.S.S.R.: Baku to Samarkand (about 900 miles)
    4. U.S.S.R.: Omsk to Samarkand (about 1100 miles)

Color Transparency 3 ■ Transmaster 1

■ Divide the class into groups. For this activity, each group will need a road atlas of the United States such as the Rand McNally *Road Atlas and Travel Guide*. The atlas should include inset maps of major cities in the United States. Give each group a copy of Transmaster 1. Have students label their state on the transmaster and make a bar scale for their maps using the following scale: $1'' = 310$ miles. Next have each group pick a state and city for which maps can be found in the reference atlas. Each group will need three maps for comparison: Transmaster 1, a state map, and a city map. Ask students which map shows the largest land area? the smallest land area? Have students predict the map where one inch is likely to equal the largest number of miles (U.S.) and the smallest number of miles (city). Then have students find the scales on each of the maps. Instruct each group to make a list of four facts or pieces of information that can be obtained from studying each map. For example, from a city map students can learn locations of streets, parks, and airports. From a state map, they can learn locations of rivers, major cities, interstate highways, and places of interest. Ask each group to share its list with the class.

Color Transparency 4 ■ pages 7-8
Skill: Using a map key
■ Cover all of the map titled "Natural Vegetation of Australia" and the map key of the natural resources map. Then display **CT 4**. Judging by the map title, what do students think the symbols on the map represent? (types of natural resources) Have students speculate what specific symbols stand for. Uncover the map key and have students name the resources found near Perth (iron, silver, gold, natural gas) and Melbourne (natural gas, petroleum). What resource is most common along the east coast of Australia? (coal) west coast? (iron) Where are Australia's uranium resources? (central or middle part of the country) What are Australia's most important energy resources? (coal, natural gas, petroleum)

Uncover the vegetation map. Have students identify the subject of this map (types of trees, grass, and other plants found in different parts of Australia) and compare the map keys on the two maps. How are differences in vegetation shown on the map key? (by color) What color is used to show deserts? (orange) semi-desert or steppe? (brown) What type of vegetation is found near Darwin? (mixed broadleaf and evergreen forest) Name three other cities that have the same type of natural vegetation as Darwin. (Perth, Canberra, Adelaide, Newcastle, Sydney, Wollongong) What kind of vegetation covers the Nullarbor Plain? (steppe) the Great Artesian Basin? (grasslands) Where are Australia's tropical rain forests located? (along the northeast coast) Have students classify the following statements as true or false.

1. Cape York peninsula gets more rain than the Melbourne area. (True)
2. The northern coast receives more rain than the southern coast. (True)
3. Most people in Australia live in the middle of the country because the climate is milder. (False, central Australia appears to be the driest part of the country with a large desert area. Also, all cities on the map are along the coasts.)
4. Almost all of Australia's cities are located in areas with tropical rain forests. (False, population centers are in areas where the natural vegetation is mixed forest.)

Conclude the activity by asking students what conclusion they can draw about the relationship between natural vegetation and population, based on this map. Students might speculate that Australia's cities are located in areas which get ample rainfall, judging by the types of vegetation that grow in these areas.

Color Transparency 4 ■ Transmaster 6
■ Divide the class into groups and give each group an atlas map that shows natural vegetation in the U.S.S.R. Each group will also need a copy of Transmaster 6, colored markers, a sheet of paper, and one note card. Tell students that they will be making a natural vegetation map of the U.S.S.R. Have each group study its resource map and make a sample map key on a sheet of paper. Have groups decide whether they will use symbols, colors, or patterns to show vegetation zones and make suggestions for the labels for each zone. Define and discuss new or unfamiliar terms such as *tundra* and *taiga*. Have all groups label the following cities: Moscow, Vladivostok, Irkutsk, Volgograd, Kazan, Yakutsk, Leningrad, Kiev, Odessa, and Baku. When groups have completed their maps, have them write a few sentences describing the relationship between areas of natural vegetation and cities, suggested by their maps. (Most cities are in areas where forests or steppe is the natural vegetation, while few cities are in areas with tundra vegetation.)

Color Transparency 5 ■ page 12
Skill: Locating places using latitude and longitude
■ It is helpful to have a globe and a wall map of the world to introduce this activity. Before displaying CT 5, write the terms *parallels of latitude* and *meridians of longitude* on the chalkboard and discuss the meaning of these terms. Remind students that to make it easier to locate places on Earth, cartographers use a grid system made up of imaginary lines that cross each other, like the lines on graph paper. These lines are called parallels of latitude and meridians of longitude. Parallels of latitude run east and west around the world and stay the same distance apart. Distances between parallels and between meridians are measured in degrees. The equator is located at 0° latitude and is the starting point for measuring latitude. Have students find the parallel that is closest to the North Pole (90° N) and the South Pole on a globe (90° S). Meridians of longitude run north and south. They are not parallel because they all meet at the North Pole and the South Pole. The

starting point for measuring longitude is the Prime Meridian, located at 0° longitude. Have students find this line on a globe and name two countries besides England that the Prime Meridian crosses. (France, Spain, Algeria, Mali) *Meridians of longitude* are measured in degrees east or west of the Prime Meridian.

To pinpoint a location on a map, *coordinates* are used. Coordinates are the places where lines of latitude and longitude intersect, or cross. For example, Washington, D.C., is located at 38° N, 77° W. The first coordinate is the latitude of Washington, D.C. and the second coordinate is the longitude. Display **CT 5**. Ask students what country is shown on the map. (Denmark) Have volunteers name several meridians and parallels shown on the map. Point out that unlike most maps students will see, this map shows a line for each degree of longitude or latitude. Then have volunteers circle the cities closest to each of these pairs of coordinates:

1. 57° N, 10° E (Alborg)
2. 56° N, 8° E (Ringkobing)
3. 55° N, 9° E (Abenra)

Inform students that while degrees of latitude and longitude are used to help pinpoint locations, sometimes a more exact description is needed. For example, the Danish city of Viborg is between 56° N and 57° N latitude and between 9° E and 10° E longitude. To find Viborg's exact location, degrees of latitude and longitude are divided into smaller units. Each degree is divided into 60 minutes. The symbol for the minute is ′. Each minute is divided into seconds. The symbols for the seconds is ″. Using this system, the exact location of Viborg is 56° 27′ N, 9° 23′ E. Have volunteers circle the cities located at each of these coordinates:

1. 55° 41′ N, 12° 34′ E (Copenhagen)
2. 55° 57′ N, 11° 44′ E (Nykobing)
3. 55° 14′ N, 10° 35′ E (Svendborg)

Color Transparency 5 ■ Transmaster 2
■ Students will need markers and a political map of the world, showing lines of latitude and longitude. Give each student a copy of Transmaster 2 and a world map. Have students label the oceans, equator, Prime Meridian, and their state. Then put the following pairs of coordinates on the chalkboard, omitting the names of the cities in parentheses. Tell students that these coordinates mark the ten most populated cities in the world. Assist students in identifying the hemispheres in which each city is located. Instruct students to locate and label each of these cities:

1. 35° N, 139° E (Tokyo)
2. 19° S, 99° W (Mexico City)
3. 23° S, 46° W (Sao Paulo)
4. 40° N, 73° W (New York)
5. 37° N, 127° E (Seoul)
6. 34° N, 135° E (Osaka)
7. 34° S, 58° W (Buenos Aires)
8. 22° N, 88° E (Calcutta)
9. 18° N, 72° E (Bombay)
10. 22° S, 43° W (Rio de Janeiro)

Students may use the political map as a point of reference. After students have completed their maps, put the correct answers on the chalkboard. Students may correct their own maps.

Color Transparency 6 ■ page 15
Skill: Interpreting a climate map
■ Before displaying the map, remind students that latitude is closely linked to climate. Five latitude lines divide the Earth into major climate zones. These lines are the equator, the Tropic of Capricorn, the Tropic of Cancer, the Arctic Circle and the Antarctic Circle. The part of the world between the Tropic of Cancer and the Tropic of Capricorn is called the tropical zone. North and south of the tropical zone are the Earth's two temperate or moderate zones. Most places in the temperate zones have warm or hot summers and cool or cold winters. Farther from the equator, close to the North and South poles, are the polar zones that are cold year round. Point out that other factors also affect climate. For example, climates in mountain or highland regions are influenced by altitude or elevation.

Display **CT 6**. Have a volunteer explain what the topic of the map is (climate regions of South America) and locate the two special lines of latitude (equator, Tropic of Capricorn). Direct students' attention to the map key. What are the five major types of climates shown on the map? (tropical, temperate, polar, dry, highlands) Have students name two cities with a highlands climate (La Paz, Sucre) and explain how the climates in Brasilia and Rio de Janeiro are alike (both tropical) and different (Rio de Janeiro hot and rainy all year. Brasilia has a rainy season and a dry season.) What city is closest to the Tropic of Cancer?

(Rio de Janeiro) What type of climate do most parts of the countries between the equator and the Tropic of Capricorn have? (tropical)

Conclude by having students decide whether these statements are true or false.

1. La Paz, Bolivia has a hotter climate than Valparaiso, Chile. (False, La Paz has a highlands climate. Valparaiso has a desert climate.)
2. Cape Horn gets more rain than Brasilia. (True)
3. Latitude is a more important factor in the climate of Quito, Peru than altitude. (False, altitude appears to be more important because Quito has a highlands climate despite the fact that it is on the equator within the tropical climate zone.)

Color Transparency 6 ■ Transmaster 4

■ Divide the class into five groups. Assign each group one of the following areas: Greenland, Canada, the United States, Mexico, and Central America. For this activity, each group will need markers, one note card, and a climate map showing the climate zones in either Central America, the United States, Canada, or Greenland. Give each group a copy of Transmaster 4. Have all groups label the following: the equator, the Tropic of Capricorn, the Tropic of Cancer, Mexico, Canada, Greenland, the United States, Central America, Pacific Ocean, Atlantic Ocean, and Arctic Ocean. Before distributing the climate maps, ask each group to write a paragraph describing the types of climates they think they will find in the area assigned to them. You may list the five climate types on the chalkboard: tropical, temperate, dry, highlands, and polar. In writing their paragraphs, students should draw on what they have learned about the relationship between latitude and climate. Groups can examine their maps and identify the lines of latitude that fall within their specific area.

After students have made their predictions, distribute the climate maps. Have students make climate maps for the different areas. When maps are completed, students may check their predictions against their completed maps. Ask students to note reasons for inaccurate predictions such as presence of unknown mountain ranges in areas believed to be within a tropical zone. Have each group write a second paragraph correctly describing the climate in the area assigned to them based on the information on their maps.

Color Transparency 7 ■ page 16
Skill: Using a letter-number grid

■ Display CT 7. Ask students what kind of place is shown on this map—city, state, or country. (city) Then tell the class that this is a map of the city of Canterbury, a city southeast of London in the United Kingdom. Point to the letters and numbers along the bottom and side of the map and ask students what type of map this is. (grid map) Tell students that the alphabetical list of all the place names on the map is called an index. Remind students that this type of map is read by using coordinates made up of a letter and a number to locate places. For example, Pin Hill is located near coordinates E-2. Judging by the index, in what part of Canterbury are most points of interest located? (north, northeast) Cover the index with a note card and ask volunteers to circle the places of interest located at the following coordinates: D-4 (Bus Station), A-2 (Falstaff Inn), B-2 (Westgate Gardens) and write the coordinates for these streets: Station Road East (E-2), North Lane (A-2), St. Martin's Road (7-C). Then have students use the scale to determine the approximate distance from the Falstaff Inn to the Weaver's Cottage (1/8 mile) and from Wincheap Green to Christchurch Cathedral (3/8 mile).

Uncover the index. Have a volunteer locate and circle Wincheap Green and the Falstaff Inn on the map. Then ask all students to take out a sheet of paper and write a set of instructions for the shortest route from Wincheap Green to the Falstaff Inn. Instructions should use compass directions and names of specific streets. (Go northeast on Castle Street, then northwest on High Street. Follow High Street until it changes into St. Peer's Street. Falstaff Inn will be on the north side of the street after the Information Center.) Ask a student to read his or her directions aloud, while a volunteer traces the path indicated on the map. Repeat this procedure asking students to write directions for each of the following items:

1. from St. Martin's Church to Pin Hill
2. from the post office to Military Road
3. from King's School to East Railroad Station

In some cases, students will have several different routes to the same place. Conclude by dividing the class into groups. Ask each group to plan a walking tour of Canterbury that includes visits to at least six points of interest shown on the map. Instruct each group to write a set of directions for the tour guide.

Color Transparency 7 ■ Transmaster 1

■ Divide the class into pairs. Each pair will need a political map of the United States, a ruler, one note card, and one sheet of paper. Give each group a copy of Transmaster 1. To begin this activity, have groups use a ruler and markers to turn their transmasters into letter-number grid maps. Starting at the bottom left-hand corner of the map, students can use their rulers to mark off 1 inch spaces along each of the four borders of the map. At each of the marks, have students put letters along the left side of the page and numbers along the bottom. Next have students locate and label twenty state capitals. Encourage students to spread their choices across the map rather than putting all of them in the same part of the country. After capitals are labeled, have students create indexes for their maps on a separate sheet of paper. Also, have each pair make a list of the grid locations of five capitals and a second list of the names of five states. Have groups exchange maps and note cards, but not indexes. Ask each group to find the names of the capitals on the note cards they have received, using the grid locations as a guide and circle these cities on their maps. Then ask groups to list the coordinates where each state listed on their note card appears. For example, most of North Carolina falls within D-8. Students can then return maps and note cards to their owners and check the accuracy of their responses.

Color Transparency 8 ■ page 21
Skill: Reading a contour map

■ Review the term elevation. Tell students that elevation is the height of land measured above or below sea level. There are different ways to show elevation. One way to show elevation on a map is to use contour lines for different elevations. CT 8 is a contour map. It uses contour lines to show elevation. Display CT 8. On a contour map the viewer is looking down on the land from above. Contour lines show the height of land. All points along the same contour line are at the same height, or elevation. For example, all the places on the line labeled 4000 are at 4000 feet above sea level. Locate point B on the map. Tell students that its elevation is between 2500 and 3000 feet.

Explain that contour lines that are close together show elevation that increases sharply, as in climbing a steep hill. When contour lines are farther apart, the slope of the land is not as steep. Have a volunteer find two mountains (near points A and B) and mark the highest points on these mountains. Is the mountain near Point A or Point B higher? (near point B) How much higher? (1000 feet) Would the northern or the southern slope of the mountain close to Point A be harder to climb? (northern) Why? (It has a steeper slope as indicated by how close the contour lines are to each other.) Direct students' attention to the map key and have students note the location of the river, old road, new road, and tunnel. Ask a volunteer to draw an arrow showing the direction in which the river flows. (downhill from north to south) At what elevation is the tunnel located? (slightly over 2500 feet) Are the old road and the new road at the same elevation? (No, the new road goes through the mountain at a little over 2500 feet. The old road crosses the mountain between 2000 and 2500 feet.)

Conclude by asking students in what direction they would be walking if they went from the first point in each pair to the second:

1. from Point A to the mouth of the river (downhill)
2. from Point C to Point B (uphill)
3. from Point B to Point A (downhill, uphill, downhill)

Color Transparency 8 ■ Transmaster 7

■ Divide the class into groups. Each group will need modeling clay, poster board, rulers, and a copy of Transmaster 7. All groups will also need a physical map of Canada from an atlas or encyclopedia. Instruct students to label all the provinces shown on the map and then identify major mountain ranges in Canada. Have groups mark these locations on Transmaster 7. (The mountain ranges students can identify are the Rocky Mountains, Coast Mountains, and Laurentian Highlands.) Then have each group tape their marked transmaster securely onto another piece of poster board. Instruct students to use the modeling clay to "build" mountains on the transmaster at each mountain range location they marked on their maps. Have groups display and compare finished mountain range maps.

Color Transparency 9 ■ page 22
Skill: Using an elevation map

■ Display **CT 9**. Ask students to identify the place shown on the map. (Africa) Next ask students what the subject of this map is. (elevation of Africa) How is elevation shown on this map? (by color) Examine the map key. What is the lowest elevation shown? (below sea level) the highest? (10,000 feet and over) Make sure students understand that the different colored areas represent a range in elevation. Have students decide which place in each pair is at a higher elevation.

1. Ethiopia, Senegal (Ethiopia)
2. Morocco, Somalia (Morocco)
3. Zambia, Ghana (Zambia)
4. western Sudan, eastern Sudan (western)
5. Angola Plateau, Ahaggar Plateau (same elevation)

Tell students that Africa is sometimes called the "plateau continent." Why do students think it has this name? A comparison of CT 9 with elevation maps of Europe, South Africa, or Asia will help students appreciate the uniformity in the African terrain.

Color Transparency 9 ■ Transmaster 5

■ Divide the class into groups. Students will need markers, an elevation or physical map of Europe, and copies of Transmaster 5. Using maps of Europe as a guide, ask each group to make an elevation map of this continent. All groups should use the same colors to identify elevations in their map keys. CT 9 may be displayed and used as a model. When groups have completed their maps, ask each group to write ten true-false statements about the information shown on the map. Statements can be based on comparisons of elevations of two cities (Madrid is at a higher elevation than Lisbon.); of two countries (Finland is more mountainous than Norway.); or of parts of the same country (The flattest area of France is along its western coast.) Have groups exchange statements and mark each statement true or false, correcting false statements.

Color Transparency 10 ■ pages 24–25
Skill: Identifying map projections

■ Remind students that the Earth is a sphere and a globe is the only true model of the Earth. When map makers make a flat map of the Earth, not all of the Earth's curved surface is shown quite accurately. To make a flat picture of the Earth, map makers must change the sizes and shapes of lands and oceans. These changes are called *distortions*. The more of Earth's surface a map shows, the more it has been flattened out and the greater its distortions. Maps of the whole world show the most distortion and maps of small areas show the least. Different ways of drawing the Earth on a flat surface are called *projections*. Different projections are useful for different purposes. One projection may distort the size of a continent, but show distances accurately. Another might show shape and distance correctly but distort size.

Display **CT 10**. It shows two projections. The circular projection is called a polar projection because it shows the Earth as if you were looking down at the North Pole. Another polar projection could show the Earth from looking down at the South Pole. Which pole is at the center of this projection? (North Pole) What are the lines that intersect at the center of the map? (meridians of longitude) Have a volunteer locate parallels shown on this map. Are these parallels north or south of the equator? (north) Which hemisphere is shown on this map? (northern) Which continents are not shown on this map? (Antarctica, Australia)

The other projection is a Mollweide projection. It is an equal-area projection which means that an area of one part of the Earth is shown in correct proportion to an area of another part of the Earth. For example, South America is about nine times the area of Greenland. This relationship is reflected on a Mollweide projection. However, to achieve equality of area, shapes are distorted, especially near the edges of the map. Ask students which projection might be used for each of the following:

1. to decide on the fastest airplane route over the North Pole (polar)
2. to show climate regions of the world (Mollweide)
3. to compare population distribution in different parts of the world (Mollweide)
4. to show the southern hemisphere (polar)
5. to show life expectancy worldwide (Mollweide)

Color Transparency 10 ■ Transmasters 10 and 11

■ Arrange the students in small groups. Each group will need scissors, blue, purple, and brown markers, tape, and a sphere of some kind about the size of an orange. Distribute Transmaster 10. Ask students what kind of a projection this is. (polar) Which pole is at the center of this projection? (North Pole) Note the meridians of longitude on the map. Have students label the Prime Meridian and the Arctic Circle. What meridians pass through the North Pole? (all) Have students label all continents, Greenland, and all oceans. CT 10 may be displayed to serve as a reference.

Distribute Transmaster 11. Tell students that to draw a map of the Earth, map makers imagine they are peeling back the surface of the globe and flattening it out. It is like trying to peel an orange in one piece. Once this "peel" of Earth is placed on a flat surface, the map makers must stretch and tear it to make it lay flat. The "peel" of the Earth resembles Transmaster 11. Have students locate the meridians and parallels on this map. How are the meridians on this "orange peel" map different from the meridians on Transmaster 10? (They are parallel to each other rather than intersecting at the poles.) Have students use a purple marker to mark the equator on Transmaster 11. Then ask students to cut out the map on Transmaster 11, making sure it stays in one piece. Students can hold the "peel" loosely around the sphere so that they can see its relationship to a globe. Note that when placed around the sphere, meridians meet at the poles. Then using Transmaster 10 as a guide, have students color the portions of Transmaster 11 that would also be found on a polar projection centered on the North Pole. Oceans should be blue and continents brown. Remind students to color only the portions of the "orange peel" that are shown on Transmaster 10. When students have finished coloring the "orange peel," it can be taped around the sphere and compared with the polar projection on Transmaster 10.

Conclude by comparing sizes and shapes of continents on both maps, looking for areas of distortions. As a follow-up activity, groups might try making sketches of a polar projection centered on the South Pole, using the uncolored portion of Transmaster 11 as a guide.

Color Transparency 11 ■ page 27
Skill: Finding routes and distance using a highway map

■ Display **CT 11**. Have a student read the title of this map and discuss what it shows. (highways in Central Chile) Point to the map key. What three types of roads are shown on this map? (major roads, other roads, paths) What part of the country has the most roads? (west coast) Which area has the fewest roads going north-south? (eastern Chile) Point out that on many highway maps, numbers are used to designate different types of highways. What symbols are used on this map? (colors, line width, dots) What type of road connects Cureoto and Constitution? (path) Santiago and Valparaiso? (major road) What part of the country has the most major roads? (northeast) Why? (The capital, Santiago, is located in the northeast.) Point to the many symbols that look like brackets along several of the paths that cross the border between Chile and Argentina. Have students speculate what these symbols represent. (bridges)

Conclude by asking students to compute the distance from Santiago to Curico (120 miles) and from Santiago to Volcan Maipo (80 miles). Which place is the shorter distance from Santiago in measured miles? (Volcan Maipo) Which would probably be closer in travel time? (Curico, because there are better roads between Santiago and Curico othan between Santiago and Volcan Maipo.)

Color Transparency 11 ■ Transmaster 5

■ For this activity, divide students into five groups. Each group will need a map that shows major cities and highways in Europe. The Rand McNally *Road Atlas of Europe* is a good resource. Give each group a copy of Transmaster 5 and assign each group one of the following countries:

1. France: Paris, Bordeaux, Lyon, Marseille, Toulouse
2. Spain: Madrid, Cartagena, Bilbao, Barcelona, Valencia
3. Italy: Rome, Milan, Naples, Venice, Turin, Genoa
4. United Kingdom: London, Birmingham, Manchester, Dover, Reading
5. West Germany: Bonn, Berlin, Frankfurt, Hamburg, Stuttgart

Have each group make a highway map for their assigned country. The map should show the capital city, the other cities listed, and the major highways and other roads that connect these cities with the national capital. Students may compare maps and determine traffic patterns.

Color Transparency 12 ■ page 28
Skill: Reading a city map

■ Display **CT 12.** Ask students if the area shown on the map is a country, state or city. (city) How can students tell? (amount of detail, streets, parks) Tell students that this is a city map of Vancouver, a city in the province of British Columbia, Canada. Have students locate Vancouver on a wall map of Canada or North America. Point to the map key and have students name different types of highways shown on the map. What type of highway is Highway 7? (four-lane divided highway) Highway 1? (limited access) What are two points of interest on 4th Avenue? (Hastings Mill Store Museum, Maritime Museum, and Planetarium) In what part of Vancouver are most of the major points of interest located? (northeast) Ask students to find the distance from New Westminister to Burnaby (about 4 miles) and from Port Coquitlam to Maple Ridge (about 11 miles).

Next have volunteers take turns giving directions from the first place in each pair below to the second, while a second student traces the route on CT 12.
1. West Vancouver to Bear Creek Park (Go southeast on Marine Drive about 5 1/2 miles, then southeast on Highway 1 about 16 miles or 9 exits, then west on 104th Avenue one block, then south on King George Highway about 2 1/2 miles. Bear Creek Park will be on the east side of the street.)
2. Richmond to the Zoo (Go northeast on No. 3 Road about 1 1/4 miles, then northwest across the Fraser River on Highway 99, then north on Granville Street about 5 1/2 miles, then northwest on Highway 1A/99 about 1 mile. The zoo will be on the east side of the street.)
3. Port Coquitlam to Central Park (Go southwest on Brunette Avenue about 5 miles, then west on Highway 1 about 4 exits or 7 miles to Boundary Road, then south on Boundary Road about one block to the intersection of Kingsway and Boundary. Central Park will be on the east side of the street.)

Color Transparency 12 ■ Transmaster 1

■ Divide the class into groups. For this activity students will need a road atlas, such as the Rand McNally *Road Atlas and Travel Guide,* markers, and copies of Transmaster 1. Write the following list of national parks on the chalkboard:
1. Everglades, FL
2. Great Smoky Mountains, TN/NC
3. Carter Lake, OR
4. Carlsbad Caverns, NM
5. Mammoth Cave, KY
6. Grand Teton, WY
7. Yellowstone, ID
8. Yosemite, CA
9. Grand Canyon, AZ
10. Mount Rainier, WA

Tell students to imagine that they are leading a tour of the national parks in the United States. It will be a bus tour which begins and ends in Miami, Florida. It is the responsibility of the tour leaders to plan the highway route for the tour. The bus will stop at each of the national parks listed, but the order in which the stops are made will depend on the tour organizers. Have students use their atlases to locate each park on their transmasters and chart a route of travel for the tour. Have students display their tour maps and explain the route they chose.

Color Transparency 13 ■ pages 34–35
Skill: Comparing historical maps

■ Display **CT 13.** Ask students what kinds of maps these are. (historical maps) One important way these maps differ from other types of maps is that they describe an area as it looked in the past rather than the present. What part of the world is shown on these maps? (Europe) What time periods are shown? (1810 and 1815) Tell students that between 1800 and 1810 Napoleon Bonaparte built an empire that included most of Europe. However, between 1812 and 1815, Napoleon's empire crumbled. Direct students' attention to the map of 1810. Have students examine the map key and name the areas that were ruled by Napoleon (Naples, Italy, Switzerland, Spain, Warsaw) and allied with Napoleon (Norway and Denmark, Prussia, Austrian Empire, Russian Empire). Which area opposed Napoleon? (United Kingdom) What countries were

neutral? (Portugal, Ottoman Empire, Sardinia, Sicily, Sweden) Next direct students' attention to the map of 1815. What does the solid red line in the center of Europe represent? (the borders of the German Confederation) Locate the "boot" of Italy on the map and ask students to describe what happened to France's empire on the Italian peninsula. (became the Papal States and Tuscany) Who claimed the portion of the French Empire that shared an eastern border with the Ottoman and Austrian empires in 1810? (Austrian Empire)

Have volunteers describe the changes that took place in each of the following countries between 1810 and 1815:
1. Kingdom of Naples (became the kingdom of the Two Sicilies, adding the island of Sicily)
2. Kingdoms of Norway and Denmark (Denmark became independent, Sweden and Norway united.)
3. Prussia (expanded to include Grand Duchy of Warsaw and part of the Confederation of the Rhine)
4. France (northern portion became independent as Netherlands, southeastern portion added to the Kingdom of Sardinia)
5. Grand Duchy of Warsaw (most of it added to the Russian Empire, northwestern portion added to Prussia)

Color Transparency 13 ■ Transmaster 5

■ Display **CT 13** and give each student a copy of Transmaster 5. Students will also need a political map of modern Europe. Have students label the countries of Europe and then make a chart comparing Europe in 1815 and Europe today. Ask students to label the columns as follows: Countries Existing in 1815 Only, Countries Existing Today Only, Countries Existing in 1815 and Today. After students have completed their charts, each student can write a paragraph summarizing the changes that have taken place in Italy, Germany, and the Ottoman Empire since 1815.

Color Transparency 14 ■ page 39
Skill: Using a special purpose map

■ Display **CT 14** and remind students that winds move across the surface of the ocean, causing *ocean currents*, bodies of sea water which flow along a path through the ocean. Warm currents are currents that carry heated water from the low latitudes into the cooler high latitudes. Cold currents carry cooled water from the higher latitudes to the lower latitudes. How are warm water currents shown on the map? (red arrows) cool currents? (blue arrows) What is name of the current that flows along the eastern coast of the United States? (Gulf Stream) the western coast of Europe? (Gulf Stream) What current influences the climate in Sydney? (Australia) How does it influence the climate in Sydney? (contributes to warmer weather) Judging by this map, would Sydney, Australia or Santiago, Chile be cooled by ocean currents? (Santiago)

Conclude by having a volunteer find the equator on the map. Explain to students that low latitudes are parallels that are close to the equator, in the tropical zones. High latitudes are parallels closer to the poles in the polar zones. With this information in mind, have students study the map and discuss the following statements that describe characteristics of ocean currents. Volunteers can find examples on the map and also note exceptions to each statement.
1. Currents generally flow in circular paths.
2. Cold currents flow from higher latitudes to lower latitudes.
3. Warm currents flow from lower latitudes to higher latitudes.
4. Currents flow clockwise in the Northern Hemisphere.
5. Currents flow counterclockwise in the Southern Hemisphere.

Color Transparency 14 ■ Transmaster 8

■ For this activity students will need markers and a time zone map that shows standard time zones and areas with nonstandard times as well. Areas with nonstandard time are areas where time varies from standard time by half an hour or more. Distribute Transmaster 8 and ask students what kind of special purpose map it is. (time zone map) Review and discuss other special purpose maps, such as the World Ocean Currents Map on CT 14. Remind students that time zones are not all evenly spaced, but are extended in some areas to include all parts of the same state or country (Greenland, for example) or to make time zones the same as those of neighboring states or countries (Bolivia and Chile). Moving from east to west, the time becomes one hour earlier as you enter each new zone. Have students identify the time zone in which their state is located and color all land areas that fall within this time zone the same color. Ask students to use a second color to label and color all countries with nonstandard time zones. This information can be found on time zone reference maps. Have students give their maps titles and make map keys. Students can also label the Soviet Union, Canada, the United States, and Brazil and count the number of times zones within each. (11, 7, 6, 3)

Color Transparency 15 ■ page 42
Skill: Comparing population maps
■ Display **CT 15**. Give students several minutes to study the two maps. Have students compare countries such as Canada, Australia, the Soviet Union, and Italy. Then explain to students that the map at the top of the page is called a *cartogram*. Cartograms show data that might otherwise be presented in chart or graph form, such as data about population, life expectancy, or economic indicators. The cartogram on CT 15 shows the land area of countries in proportion to their populations. The more people a country has, the bigger the country looks on the map. The map at the bottom of CT 15 is an equal-area map that shows the true size and shape of the countries of the world for comparison. Have students use the cartogram and the equal-area map to decide which of the countries in each pair has a larger population in proportion to its land area: Soviet Union or China (China); Peru or Bolivia (Peru); East Germany or West Germany (West Germany); Bangladesh or Pakistan (Bangladesh). Which continent has the largest population? (Asia) the smallest? (Australia) Why isn't Antarctica shown on the cartogram? (No people live there.)

Ask students which of the following are true and which are false.
1. Population is evenly distributed throughout the world. (False)
2. Alaska's population greatly exceeds its land area. (False)
3. South Korea is more crowded than North Korea. (True)
4. Mongolia is sparsely settled. (True)
5. The population of the Western Hemisphere is greater than the population of the Eastern Hemisphere. (False)

Color Transparency 15 ■ Transmaster 3
■ For this activity students will need population data on the countries of the Eastern Hemisphere, colored markers, and a political map showing the countries of the Eastern Hemisphere. Divide students into groups. Inform students that they will be making a population map of the Eastern Hemisphere. This map will use color to show population. Have students label all countries shown on CT 15 and indicate population with color, following these key guidelines:
Less than 15 million people: no color
15 million to 40 million people: blue
40 million to 65 million people: green
65 million to 100 million people: yellow
100 million to 500 million people: orange
Over 500 million people: red
When all groups have completed their maps, display CT 15. Have students compare the two maps, discussing the advantages and disadvantages of each type of map for showing population data.

Color Transparency 16 ■ page 46
Skill: Finding the best route
■ Display **CT 16**. Tell students that this is a road map for the Canadian province of Manitoba. Point out that this is also a grid map. Have students find the grid locations of Winnipeg (G–4), Swan River (D–1), Grand Rapids (C–2), and Flin Flon (A–1). Students can also identify the most direct route from the first point in each pair to the second point:
1. Winnipeg to Grand Rapids (Go north on Highway 6.)
2. Manigotagan to Portage La Prairie (Go south on 304, then southwest on 59 to Winnipeg, then west on Highway 1.)
3. Flin Flon to Riverton (Go south on Highway 10, then east on Highway 60 to Highway 6. Turn south on Highway 6 to Ashern, then east on Highway 325 to Highway 234, and south on Highway 234.)

Show students the red pointers and numbers on the map and explain that the numbers between each pair of pointers indicate distances between major cities. Circle Winnipeg and Falcon Lake and have students read the mileage between these two cities (85 miles) and between Brandon and Virden (49 miles). What city is 76 miles south of Swan River? (Roblin) Have students describe three alternate routes from Dauphin to Swan River. Which is the fastest? (north on Highway 10) Which would probably be the most scenic? (north on Highway 366 through Duck Mountain Provincial Park)

Color Transparency 16 ■ Transmaster 7
■ Divide students into seven groups. For this activity, each group will need a highway map of Canada such as the Rand McNally *Road Atlas and Travel Guide*. Tell students that the 5000-mile Trans-Canada Highway is the longest highway in the world. This highway connects the eastern and western coasts of Canada. Display CT 16. Ask a volunteer to locate this highway on the map. (Highway 1) Tell students that in the eastern provinces this highway is Highway 17. In Quebec it is Highway 20. Assign each group one of the following provinces of Canada: Alberta, British Columbia, Ontario, Quebec, New Brunswick, Manitoba, or Saskatchewan. Ask groups to label the following for the province assigned to them: provincial capital, two cities on the Trans-Canada Highway, one provincial or national park, and all large bodies of water. Then ask students to draw the portion of the Trans-Canada Highway that runs through their province. Students can also draw one highway or road connecting each city on the map with the provincial capital. Road and highway numbers should be indicated on their maps.

Color Transparency 17 ■ page 48
Skill: Comparing special purpose maps
■ Display **CT 17**. Discuss what land-use maps show. (where crops and animals are raised, where mineral resources are located, and locations of major centers of manufacturing) Then ask: Where is all of the farm land in Egypt located? (along the Nile River) What category of land covers the largest area in Egypt? (land too dry for farming) What are the major land uses in Spain? (farm land, grazing) In what part of Spain are olives and citrus fruit grown? (east and southeast) What kinds of livestock are raised in Spain? (sheep, hogs, cattle) in Egypt? (sheep, goats, cattle) Judging by the map, in which country is raising livestock a more important economic activity? (Spain, grazing is an important land use and symbols for livestock are more numerous.) Which country has more iron? (Spain) more oil? (Egypt)

Have students decide which country each of the statements describes. Some statements apply to both countries.
1. The country that has a greater variety of mineral resources. (Spain)
2. Most of this country's land cannot be used for farming. (Egypt)
3. The country that has only a few manufacturing centers. (Both)
4. Fishing is an important land use in coastal areas. (Both)
5. Dates are raised in dry areas. (Egypt)

Color Transparency 17 ■ Transmaster 9
■ Divide students into an even number of groups. Groups will need land-use maps of North Africa or Southwest Asia. Such maps are found in atlases and geography textbooks. Ask a volunteer to locate Egypt on a wall map of the world. Ask volunteers to name the countries that border Egypt to the east, west, and south. (Libya, Israel, Sudan) Judging by the land-use map of Egypt on CT 17, what types of land use would students expect to find in the countries that border Egypt? Would students expect land uses to be similar to those of Egypt or Spain? Have students write answers to these questions and discuss responses.

Assign one of the following countries to each group: Morocco, Algeria, Libya, Saudi Arabia, Turkey, Iran, Iraq, and Israel. Distribute copies of Transmaster 9 and ask each group to make a land use map for their assigned country. The map should show major land uses, manufacturing centers, and important crops and mineral resources. When all groups have completed their maps, display CT 17. Ask each group to write two or three paragraphs comparing the land uses in Egypt and the land uses in the country assigned. Ask a spokesperson for each group to read the paragraphs aloud.

Color Transparency 18 ■ page 57
Skill: Comparing circle graphs
■ Display **CT 18**. Ask students what types of graphs these are. (circle graphs) Remind students that circle graphs can be used to show and compare the parts of a whole. Each section of the circle stands for a fractional part or percentage of the whole or 100 percent. The topic of CT 18 is the division of GNP in Denmark, Hungary, and Egypt. GNP or *gross national product* is the total value of the goods and services that a country produces in a year. Goods include farm products such as grain and meat and factory goods such as steel and automobiles. Services include businesses

such as banking, insurance, and restaurants. Ask students what percentage of the GNP in Denmark comes from farming (6%) and from industry (27%). In which country do services contribute the largest share to the GNP? (Denmark) In which of these three countries does farming make the greatest contribution to the GNP? (Egypt)

Have students name the country or countries best described by each of the following statements.
1. Industry contributes almost half of the GNP. (Hungary)
2. Services contribute more than 2/3 of the GNP. (Denmark)
3. Almost half of the GNP comes from service-related activities. (Egypt)
4. Industry and agriculture combined contribute less to the GNP than services. (Denmark)
5. Agriculture contributes least to the GNP. (all)

Color Transparency 18 ■ Transmaster 12
■ In this activity students will make circle graphs like those in CT 18 containing economic information on the division of GNP in three countries—Tanzania, Burma, and the United States. Write the following information on the chalkboard:

Burma: 48% (agriculture), 13% (industry), 39% (services)
Tanzania: 59% (agriculture), 10% (industry), 31% (services)
United States: 2% (agriculture), 31% (industry), 67% (services)
Distribute Transmaster 12 and ask all students to make three circle graphs, one for each country. Students can begin by estimating the fractions into which each circle will be divided. Students may draw their graphs, labeling each section. After students have completed their graphs, the graphs can be compared with each other and with CT 18. Students can also make up descriptive statements like those in the activity for CT 18 and discuss their answers.

Color Transparency 19 ■ page 59
Skill: Comparing bar graphs
■ Display **CT 19**. Ask students what kind of graphs these are. (bar graphs) Point out that these are horizontal bar graphs. Have a volunteer read the titles and tell what they are about. (The amount of gold and silver mined in major producing nations.) Explain that gold and silver are usually measured in troy ounces which are slightly heavier than ordinary ounces. Check students' ability to read the graph by asking volunteers to name the countries that were first in gold (Mexico) and silver (South Africa) production. How much silver did Mexico produce? (about 53 million troy ounces) Judging by these graphs which is the more rare or precious metal—gold or silver? (gold, less is mined) Which country produces more silver—Canada or the United States? (United States) How much more? (about 6 million troy ounces)

Conclude by asking students to write statements which use the information on the graphs to describe each of the following:
1. the position of South Africa in gold and silver production (South Africa is first in gold production and last in silver production.)
2. how Peru and the Soviet Union compare in silver production (Peru produces slightly more silver than the Soviet Union.)
3. the position of Australia in gold and silver production (Australia is last in gold production and sixth in silver production.)

Color Transparency 19 ■ Transmaster 2
■ For this activity students will need two different-colored markers and a world political map. Display CT 19. Using this information as a guide, have students make maps showing the areas where gold and silver are produced worldwide and include the amount of gold and silver each country produces. Have students make map keys and titles for their maps. When maps are completed, examine the advantages and disadvantages of presenting this data on bar graphs as opposed to on maps. Which do students find easier to read? What generalizations, if any, can be made about the location of the Earth's gold and silver resources from looking at the world map of these resources?

Color Transparency 20 ■ page 60
Skill: Reading a double bar graph
■ Cover the graphs of West Germany and the United States and display **CT 20**. Tell students that this is a double bar graph. Another name for this type of graph is a *population pyramid*. These graphs are used to show how a nation's population is distributed both by age group and by sex. What color is used to

show males on this graph? (green) females? (yellow) The bars on the graph represent age groups. Have a volunteer locate the bars that represent people 75 to 79 years old and 20 to 24 years old. Note that the bars are arranged in order from youngest to oldest. Point to the horizontal axis. Explain that it shows the percentage of the total population within each age group. For example, slightly less than 7% of Mexico's female population is 5 to 9 years old. Have volunteers identify the age group most students in the class belong to. (10–14) Point out that the pyramid narrows at the top. What conclusion can students draw about the birth and death rates in Mexico, from looking at the shape of its population pyramid? (The birth rate is high and the death rate is high.)

Uncover the rest of CT 20. In what years were people in the age group from 10 to 14 born? (1975–79) Tell students that in the years after World War II, the United States experienced a baby boom. Ask a volunteer to color in the area on the U.S. graph that represents the baby boom. How long did the baby boom period last? (1945–1964) Did West Germany experience a baby boom? If so, in what years did it occur? (1960–1969)

Conclude by asking students to identify the country described by each phrase:
1. smallest percentage of population under 15 years of age (West Germany)
2. highest birth rate (Mexico)
3. largest percentage of population in the age group from 30 to 39 (U.S.)
4. more women than men over the age of 65 (all)
5. smallest percentage of the population over 60 years of age (Mexico)

Color Transparency 20 ■ Transmaster 12
■ Distribute copies of Transmaster 12. Then copy the following data on the chalkboard.

	Nigeria	Mexico	United States	West Germany
Life Expectancy	51 years	68 years	75 years	75 years
Infant Mortality	104 deaths	48 deaths	10 deaths	9 deaths
Population Growth Rate	3.3%	2.1%	1%	−0.2%

Tell students that *life expectancy* is the average number of years newborn babies in a particular country can expect to live if health conditions remain the same. *Infant mortality* is the number of infants, out of every 1,000 babies born in a given year, who die before reaching one year of age. The lower the number, the fewer the infant deaths. The *population growth rate* is the rate of increase in a country's population during a one-year period. It is expressed as a percentage and reflects the number of births and deaths during the one-year period. When the growth rate is zero, births and deaths are equal. When the growth rate is a negative number or percentage, deaths exceed births.

Instruct students to make three graphs displaying this information. As a class, decide whether bar, line, or circle graphs would display the information best. (bar) Discuss the labels for the horizontal and vertical axes for each bar graph and have students complete their graphs. Students may compare these graphs with the population pyramids on CT 20 and look for relationships between the information.

Color Transparency 21 ■ page 63
Skill: Using a double-line graph
■ Display **CT 21**. Ask students what kind of graph it is (double-line graph). What does this line graph show? (average monthly temperatures in Paris and Mexico City) What is the time span shown on the graph? (12 months) What information does the map key provide? (identifies cities by color) Have a volunteer locate each of these cities on a world map, noting the latitudes within which each falls. Then ask: In what month is the temperature highest in each city? (Mexico City: May; Paris: July, August) In what month is the temperature lowest in each city? (January) In what months are the temperatures in both cities similar? (July, August, September)

Tell students that the Patterson family lives in Boston. They want to take a winter vacation to get away from the cold and snowy weather. Which city should they visit? (Mexico City) What month should they go? (February for the warmest weather) What might be the best time of year for the Pattersons to visit Paris? Have students give reasons for their opinions.

Color Transparency 21 ■ Transmaster 12

■ Divide the class into pairs. Students will need data on monthly average temperatures for cities in the United States. This information can be found in a world almanac. Distribute a copy of Transmaster 12 to each group with directions to make a double-line graph showing average monthly temperatures in two U.S. cities over a one-year period. Each group should pick two cities in different parts of the country. When all groups have completed their graphs, have each pair write five questions about their graph on one note card and provide the answers to their questions on a second note card. Groups may exchange graphs and answer one another's questions.

Color Transparency 22 ■ page 64
Skill: Using a map and a graph together

■ Display **CT 22**. Ask students what country is shown on the map. (Soviet Union) What is the subject of the map? (location of ethnic groups in the U.S.S.R.) Tell students that there are more than 100 different ethnic groups in the Soviet Union. An *ethnic group* is made up of people who share common ancestry, language, customs and traditions. Have a student describe the information on the circle graph. (percentage of the Soviet population belonging to each ethnic group) What group makes up the largest percentage of the Soviet population? (Russians) What is the second largest ethnic group in the Soviet population? (Ukrainians) Ask students to name the ethnic groups that have settled most heavily in each city: Moscow (Russians), Novosibirsk (Russians), Odessa (Ukrainians), Yerevan (Armenians), and Samarkand (Uzbeks).

Conclude by asking students if they would use the map or circle graph to find the following information:
1. the smallest ethnic group in the Soviet Union (circle graph)
2. thinly settled areas in the Soviet Union (map)
3. ethnic groups living near the Black Sea (map)
4. settlement patterns of the Uzbeks (map)
5. percentage of the Soviet Union's population made up of Russians (circle graph)

Encourage students to discuss how the graph enhances map data.

Color Transparency 22 ■ Transmasters 9 and 12

■ Divide the class into groups. Each group will need a current world almanac or a copy of the World Bank *Development Data Book* and a copy of Transmasters 9 and 12. Have groups label all the countries of Southwest Asia on the map. Next have students color all Southwest Asian countries that belong to OPEC one color and all other Southwest Asian countries another color. Have students make a key for their maps. The names of countries belonging to OPEC can be found in almanacs and encyclopedias. Then have groups use almanacs to find per capita GNP data (also known as per capita income) for: Iran, Iraq, Kuwait, Libya, Saudi Arabia, Egypt, Yemen, Syria, and Israel. Have students graph this information on a bar graph showing per capita income in thousands of dollars. Ask students to compare their map and graph looking for similarities among oil-producing nations and differences between OPEC and non-OPEC members. Ask each group to write a few sentences explaining the apparent relationship between oil production and per capita income. (In general, countries that produce oil have a higher per capita income than those that do not.)

Color Transparency 23 ■ pages 66–67
Skill: Reading a time line

■ Display **CT 23**. Ask students what the topic of this time line is. (Chinese history) Write the dates 500 A.D. and 500 B.C. on the chalkboard and have a student explain the difference between these two dates. Ask students how long a period of time is covered on this time line. (3500 years) What time interval is used? (100 years) What is the first date (1500 B.C.) and event (first cities arise) on the time line? The most recent date (1990) and event? (population reaches 1 billion) Point to the words Shang, Ch'in, and Sui on the time line. Ask students what these words represent? (The dynasties, or ruling families, that have governed China at various times in its history.) How long did the Han dynasty rule China? (a little over 400 years) Continue the study of the time line with the following questions: In what century did China become a republic? (twentieth) How long after the invention of paper was the world's first book produced? (about 850 years) How long did it take for China's population to increase from 60 million to 108 million? (almost 1700 years) from 108 million to 432 million? (about 200 years) from 423 million to 1 billion? (130 years) What pattern or

trend can students find in the rate of population growth in China? (The Chinese population is increasing at a more rapid rate today than in the past.)

Color Transparency 23 ■ Transmaster 12

■ Display CT 23 and distribute copies of Transmaster 12. Students will also need rulers and encyclopedia articles listing events in the history of Japan or India. Ask each student to make a time line for either country, including at least 15 events in the country's history dating from the earliest events they can trace to the year 2000. Have students divide their time lines into one-hundred-year intervals. When students have completed their time lines, display CT 23. Have students compare all three time lines.

Color Transparency 24 ■ page 68
Skill: Reading a diagram

■ Remind students that one purpose of a diagram is to explain a process. It often shows how something works. Display **CT 24**. Ask students what the diagrams show. (systems of government in the United States and Great Britain) What is the system of government in the United States called? (presidential) What is the British system called? (parliamentary) What groups are shown on both diagrams? (voters and Executive, Legislative, Judicial branches) What symbol appears on the parliamentary system diagram only? (monarch) What is the role of the monarch in the parliamentary system? (appoints members of the House of Lords) What people do voters elect in the presidential system? (president, members of Congress) in the parliamentary system? (members of the House of Commons)

For further comparison of the diagrams, divide students into groups. Have each group make a four-column chart on a sheet of paper. Label the columns Country, Executive Branch, Legislative Branch, and Judicial Branch. List the United States and Great Britain in the first column. Then briefly review the differences in the functions of the three branches of government. Have groups complete their charts using the information on the diagrams. Begin with the executive branch, having students name the top official in each executive branch, how this person is chosen, and his or her powers and responsibilities. Repeat this process for the legislative and judicial branches. When students' charts are finished, have them write two or three paragraphs explaining the differences between a parliamentary and presidential system of government.

Color Transparency 24 ■ Transmasters 3, 4, and 9

■ Divide the class into groups. Each group will need a current world almanac and one of the three transmasters. Tell each group that it assignment is to make a map showing the system of government found in each country on its map. The group receiving Transmaster 3 should not include Africa or Southwest Asia on its map. Information for this assignment can be found in the articles about each country in the *World Almanac* or *The Statesman's Year-book*. Groups can begin by labeling all countries shown on their maps and then deciding on categories for their map keys. (Among the categories students can include are: communistic, parliamentary, democratic, monarchical, and republican.) When groups have completed their maps, display them. As a class, decide which types of government are most common in different regions of the world.

THE OFFICIAL MANCHESTER UNITED ANNUAL 2007

BEN HIBBS and **GEMMA THOMPSON**

CONTENTS

6 NOVEMBER 1986
Alex Ferguson is named manager of United, who are second bottom in the league. The Reds eventually finish in 11th place

1987/88
Hopes of a Reds' revival are raised as United finish as runners-up behind Liverpool in the League Championship

1988/89
A disappointing season sees United finish 11th

1989/90
The Reds beat Nottingham Forest 1-0 in the FA Cup third round – some say it saved Ferguson's job. United go on to win the trophy, his first in England, beating Crystal Palace 1-0 in a replay after a 3-3 draw in the final

1990/91
United win the European Cup-Winners' Cup, finish sixth in the league, but lose the League Cup final to Sheffield Wednesday

1991/92
United clinch the UEFA Super Cup and win the League Cup for the first time but let their lead in the title race slip as Leeds snatch the title

1992/93
Champions at last! New signing Eric Cantona helps Ferguson guide United to a first title in 26 years

1993/94
The stakes rise as Alex Ferguson guides the Reds to a League and FA Cup double

1994/95
Cantona's suspension hinders United. Not even Andy Cole's £7m arrival can stop Blackburn clinching the title

1995/96
Ince, Hughes and Kanchelskis are sold as Neville, Beckham, Scholes and Butt are promoted. United win a second Double

1996/97
Ferguson steers United to a fourth Premiership title, but the Reds lose to Borussia Dortmund in the Champions League semi-final

WELCOME TO
THE MANCHESTER UNITED ANNUAL

THIS IS AN EXCITING TIME FOR THE CLUB. WE HAVE A YOUNG SQUAD THAT WILL CONTINUE TO IMPROVE. THE KEY IS TO KEEP THAT GROUP TOGETHER, THAT'S OUR PLAN. THEY WILL BENEFIT FROM PLAYING WITH EXPERIENCED PLAYERS LIKE GARY NEVILLE, RYAN GIGGS, PAUL SCHOLES AND WES BROWN, WHO HAVE GROWN UP AT THE CLUB AND RISEN THROUGH THE RANKS.

We hope to see further maturity from younger players such as Cristiano Ronaldo and Wayne Rooney, who can both, one day, be regarded as the best in the world. We have high hopes for them, but they're not alone. There's a whole group of even younger players coming up through the ranks. We have a healthy future.

You have to be patient and maybe wait two or three years for them to fully develop. Players don't reach their peak at 20 or 21, they fulfil their potential at 24 or 25. We're prepared to wait and make sure they learn the right way. We don't want to rush them. With young players you can't expect consistency. Last season we experienced that, but our form in the three months at the end of 2005/06 proved to me, the players and other clubs we'll be up there come the end of the 2006/07 season. This team is getting better all the time and with our mix of youth and experience we will continue to be a force for years to come.

The blend of old and young is clear to see in this edition of the Manchester United Annual. Ole Gunnar Solskjaer, a model professional, Giuseppe Rossi and Gerard Pique, two exciting young players, sum up the balance we believe can take this club forward.

Enjoy the read.

Sir Alex Ferguson

1997/98
Reds let an 11-point lead slip to eventual champions Arsenal and end the season empty-handed

1998/99
The most successful season in United's history; a glorious Premiership, FA Cup and Champions League Treble

12 JUNE 1999
Ferguson knighted for services to football

1999-2000
Just three league defeats earns United a sixth Premiership title by a clear 18 points. The Reds also taste victory in the Inter-Continental Cup

2000/01
Reds seal a hat-trick of Championships – their seventh overall

2001/02
Third in the league but United lose on away goals against Bayer Leverkusen in the Champions League semi-final

2002/03
Reds reclaim the title – Sir Alex's eighth Premiership crown – but lose another League Cup final, this time to Liverpool

2003/04
Sir Alex wins his fifth FA Cup as United boss

2005/06
The Reds win the League Cup

6 NOVEMBER 2006
Sir Alex celebrates 20 years in charge at Old Trafford

SIR ALEX'S HONOURS

Premiership 1993, 1994, 1996, 1997, 1999, 2000, 2001, 2003
FA Cup 1990, 1994, 1996, 1999, 2004
League Cup 1992, 2006
FA Charity/Community Shield 1990 (shared) 1993, 1994, 1996, 1997, 2003
UEFA Champions League 1999
European Cup-Winners' Cup 1991
Inter-Continental Cup 1999
UEFA Super Cup 1992
Total trophies 25

SEASON REVIEW 2005/06

AUGUST 2005

Tue 9	Debreceni VSC	CL QR3	H	W 3-0
Sat 13	Everton	Prem	A	W 2-0
Sat 20	Aston Villa	Prem	H	W 1-0
Wed 24	Debreceni VSC	CL QR3	A	W 3-0
Sun 28	Newcastle United	Prem	A	W 2-0

AFTER ENDING THE 2004/05 SEASON EMPTY-HANDED, SIR ALEX FERGUSON URGED HIS UNITED SIDE TO HIT THE GROUND RUNNING AHEAD OF THE NEW CAMPAIGN. THEY DID THAT, WINNING ALL OF THE TEAM'S FIRST FIVE FIXTURES, DOMESTICALLY AND IN EUROPE.

The Champions League qualifying draw saw the Reds pitched against Hungarian champions Debreceni. Any concerns United may have had were soon eased by the three Rs – Rooney, Ronaldo and Ruud – who set Sir Alex's side on the way to a 3-0 victory at Old Trafford. The Reds made it 6-0 on aggregate when they travelled to Budapest for the second leg, Kieran Richardson and Gabriel Heinze (twice) scoring.

Nestled between the two European qualifying matches were United's opening Premiership fixtures, first came a trip to Everton and then a home clash with Aston Villa. Ruud van Nistelrooy continued his blistering start to the season with goals in both games including the winner against Villa. Wayne Rooney bagged his second of the campaign – and his first against his former club Everton – in the 2-0 win at Goodison Park.

The month ended on a high with a trip to St. James' Park to face Newcastle. Again the attacking double-act of Rooney and Ruud combined to secure the points for United with a well-deserved 2-0 victory.

KEY STATS: in August...

242,972 people watched United play

GOALS

11	0
scored	conceded

Van Nistelrooy scored the winner against Villa and Rooney scored United's first at Newcastle in the

66th minute

RUUD REBORN

After a spate of injuries disrupted the second half of his previous campaign, Ruud van Nistelrooy began the 2005/06 season like a man possessed... with goals. He opened his account in the first leg of the Champions League qualifier against Debreceni, before bagging three more in his next four games – playing a vital role in United's impressive start to the season.

SEPTEMBER 2005

Sat 10	Manchester City	Prem	H	D 1-1
Wed 14	Villarreal	CL GpD	A	D 0-0
Sun 18	Liverpool	Prem	A	D 0-0
Sat 24	Blackburn Rovers	Prem	H	L 1-2
Tue 27	Benfica	CL GpD	H	W 2-1

United's flying start to the season was soon halted as injuries and suspensions saw the Reds stutter in September, offering unbeaten Chelsea an early lead in the title race.

A two-week international break between the last fixture in August and the first match in September seemed to knock Sir Alex's men out of their winning stride. League draws with local rivals Manchester City and Liverpool and a defeat to Mark Hughes' Blackburn saw the Reds collect just two Premiership points in September.

It was a battle in the Champions League, too. Wayne Rooney's sending off for sarcastically applauding referee Kim Milton Nielsen meant United had to scrap for a 0-0 draw away to Villarreal. The Reds suffered further pain in Spain when Gabriel Heinze fell awkwardly and damaged his knee, an injury that would see him miss the rest of the season.

It took until the last game in September, the visit of Portuguese champions Benfica to Old Trafford in the Champions League, to record a victory. Even then, it wasn't easy. Ruud van Nistelrooy struck with just five minutes remaining in a nail-biting finish after Benfica midfielder Simao Sabrosa had cancelled out Ryan Giggs' opening goal. It was a tough month.

KEY STATS: in September…

17 United players played this month

442 the formation Sir Alex DEFINITELY used

22.5 was the average age of United's injury-ravaged defence against Benfica (Bardsley, Ferdinand, O'Shea and Richardson)

22,000 attendance at Villarreal's El Madrigal Stadium, United's lowest in Europe in 2005/06

Gabriel Heinze tackles Villarreal's Antonio Guayre, but he was later stretchered off with a season-ending knee injury.

SIR ALEX SAID…

'You always hope the ball falls to Ruud, particularly in Europe, where his record speaks volumes about the player he is. Ruud is the best striker I've worked with and he's in great form at the moment. He's been an important player for us in a difficult month.'

OCTOBER 2005

Sat 1	Fulham	Prem	A	W 3-2
Sat 15	Sunderland	Prem	A	W 3-1
Tues 18	Lille	CL GpD	H	D 0-0
Sat 22	Tottenham Hotspur	Prem	H	D 1-1
Wed 26	Barnet	CC Rd3	H	W 4-1
Sat 29	Middlesbrough	Prem	A	L 1-4

October promised much but in the end delivered little. The month began well enough with two wins out of two against Fulham and Sunderland. Ruud van Nistelrooy (3) and Wayne Rooney (2) were in fine form, with young striker Giuseppe Rossi also scoring against Sunderland – his first for the club on his Premiership debut.

But things went downhill from there. A 0-0 draw with Lille at Old Trafford was United's second Champions League stalemate in three games, and a red card for Paul Scholes only made things worse.

A 4-1 win over Barnet in the third round of the Carling Cup was sandwiched between two hugely disappointing games in the Premiership, which allowed Chelsea to advance 13 points ahead at the top of the table. First, the Reds dropped two crucial points at

home to Spurs, before being crushed 4-1 at Middlesbrough's Riverside Stadium.

The only plus-point from the day was Ronaldo's injury-time header, which saw United become the first team to net 1,000 Premiership goals. Sir Alex desperately needed to lift his troops for a big month in November. 'Middlesbrough hammered us,' he said. 'But the great thing about this club is that we bounce back. We have to get over this and move on.'

KEY STATS: in October...

4 players opened their goalscoring accounts for the season (Rossi, Silvestre, Miller and Ebanks-Blake)

8 players made their first start of the season during the Carling Cup victory over Barnet (Howard, Pique, Eckersley, Martin, Miller, R. Jones, Rossi, Ebanks-Blake)

12 goals were scored

263,501 people watched United play

Young striker Giuseppe Rossi celebrates with Wayne Rooney after scoring his first Premiership goal for United against Sunderland.

MILESTONE MOMENTS

Despite the disappointing results, the matches against Middlesbrough in the Premiership and Lille in the Champions League saw two United landmarks. Ronaldo's goal against Boro was United's 1000th in the Premiership, while Ryan Giggs made his 100th European appearance against the French side.

NOVEMBER 2005

Wed 2	Lille	CL GpD	A	L 0-1
Sun 6	Chelsea	Prem	H	W 1-0
Sat 19	Charlton Athletic	Prem	A	W 3-1
Tue 18	Villarreal	CL GpD	H	D 0-0
Sun 27	West Ham United	Prem	A	W 2-1
Wed 30	West Bromwich Albion	CC Rd4	H	W 3-1

KEY STATS: in November...

7 different goalscorers

312 days since Saha's last United goal

1 the minute's silence for a true legend, George Best

4:31pm Sunday 6 November – Fletcher's winner against Chelsea

56 the same minute O'Shea scored against West Ham and West Brom

November began as disappointingly as October had ended for the Reds. United followed the 4-1 hammering by Middlesbrough with a 1-0 defeat against French side Lille in Europe.

The Reds went into the crucial league clash with Chelsea just four days later with critics claiming the club was in crisis. But Sir Alex's side called on every ounce of effort and determination to produce a fantastic team performance and a 1-0 victory, thanks to Darren Fletcher's looping header after 31 minutes.

Two further Premiership victories – over Charlton and West Ham – followed either side of another disappointing Champions League outing and the surprise announcement that Roy Keane would leave the club after more than 12 magnificent years at Old Trafford. A second 0-0 draw with Villarreal in Europe, this time at home, left the Reds needing victory in their last group game against Benfica in December to guarantee a place in the knockout stages.

United capped off a rollercoaster ride in November with an emotional night at Old Trafford, as fans paid respect to George Best, who had passed away five days before. Nearly 50,000 Reds gave a moving and fitting tribute to a United legend in the 3-1 win, which saw Saha score his first goal in almost a year.

Darren Fletcher controls the ball against Chelsea. His match-winning header sent a packed Old Trafford into wild celebration in a 1-0 win over their title rivals.

MAGIC MOMENT

In a month with its fair share of ups and downs, Darren Fletcher's goal against Chelsea not only proved United could beat José Mourinho's team, but was also a release of tension – around 60,000 United fans inside Old Trafford went crazy.

DECEMBER 2005

Sat 3	Portsmouth	Prem	H	W 3-0
Wed 7	Benfica	CL GpD	A	L 1-2
Sun 11	Everton	Prem	H	D 1-1
Wed 14	Wigan Athletic	Prem	H	W 4-0
Sat 17	Aston Villa	Prem	A	W 2-0
Tues 20	Birmingham City	CC QF	A	W 3-1
Mon 26	West Bromwich Albion	Prem	H	W 3-0
Wed 28	Birmingham City	Prem	A	D 2-2
Sat 31	Bolton Wanderers	Prem	H	W 4-1

All-action midfielder Ji-sung Park strikes his first United goal.

KEY STATS: in December...

UNITED GOALS IN ALL COMPETITIONS

23 scored

7 conceded

13 of the Reds' **23** goals were scored by Ruud, Rooney or Saha

the number of times United used all three substitutes during their nine matches **8**

December was United's busiest month of the season with nine games in four weeks, but unfortunately for the Reds it featured their most disappointing moment of the campaign as they crashed out of Europe. United knew they had to win at Benfica's Stadium of Light and proceedings began brightly with a 7th-minute goal, only the second of the season from Paul Scholes. But Brazilian pair Geovanni and Beto struck soon after for the home side who held out

for a 2-1 victory. The result left the Reds bottom of Group D and saw them fail to qualify for the Champions League knockout stages for the first time in nine years.

In contrast, United remained unbeaten in the league throughout December and found the back of the net 19 times in the process. Two of those goals came from Rio Ferdinand who, after waiting three and a half years to get his name on the scoresheet, headed home twice in four games against Wigan and West Brom. Ji-sung Park also opened his goalscoring account for the Reds with United's second goal in their 3-1 Carling Cup quarter-final win at Birmingham.

Two Premiership draws against Everton and Birmingham were the only blots on United's copybook and left them 11 points behind leaders Chelsea. While no doubt glad to see the back of a trophyless 2005, the Reds celebrated the final day of the year – and Sir Alex's 64th birthday – in style with an impressive 4-1 victory over Bolton.

RIO OPENS HIS ACCOUNT

140 matches into his Old Trafford career, Rio finally tasted success in front of goal. The defender had waited three and a half years to open his United account, which he did in the 4-0 win over Wigan on 14 December. He then doubled his tally just 12 days later against West Bromwich on Boxing Day.

JANUARY 2006

Tue 3	Arsenal	Prem	A	D 0-0
Sun 8	Burton Albion	FAC Rd3	A	D 0-0
Wed 11	Blackburn Rovers	CC SF/1L	A	D 1-1
Sat 14	Manchester City	Prem	A	L 1-3
Wed 18	Burton Albion	FAC Rd3/R	H	W 5-0
Sun 22	Liverpool	Prem	H	W 1-0
Wed 25	Blackburn Rovers	CC SF/2L	H	W 2-1
Sun 29	Wolverhampton Wanderers	FAC Rd4	A	W 3-0

In-form Louis Saha evades two Burton markers in the FA Cup third round stalemate. He went on to net four goals in January.

United welcomed 2006 with a sigh of relief – 2005 was a difficult year, and it ended with an energy-draining run of matches in December.

The games kept coming in January – unfortunately, so did the frustration. First up was Arsenal, and a final visit to Highbury before the Gunners move to their new stadium. There have been some mighty United-Arsenal battles in recent years, but this goalless contest failed to frighten league-leaders Chelsea. Draws in the FA Cup against non-league Burton Albion and in the first leg of the Carling Cup semi-final against Blackburn, plus a league defeat against Manchester City, meant a poor start to 2006 for the Reds.

However, teams managed by Sir Alex never give in. Rossi (2), Saha, Richardson and Giggs did the job properly at Old Trafford in the FA Cup replay with Burton, smashing five past the visitors without reply. Then Rio Ferdinand got a late winner against Liverpool at Old Trafford, before the Reds secured a Carling Cup final place with a 2-1 semi-final second leg win over Rovers.

The month ended with a comfortable 3-0 FA Cup win over Wolves, which paired Rio and Rooney in United's injury-hit midfield.

KEY STATS: in January...

58 days saw United complete a hectic 17-match, two-month schedule

Saturday 3 o'clock kick-offs 0

4 goals in five starts for Louis Saha

2 NEW SIGNINGS

Nemanja Vidic and Patrice Evra made their debuts

substitutions made **18**

GREAT GOAL

Defenders wait three years for a goal and then three come along in a month. However, Rio's efforts against Wigan and West Brom in December were nothing compared to his match-winning, injury-time header against Liverpool in January.

FEBRUARY 2006

Wed 1	Blackburn Rovers	Prem	A	L 3-4
Sat 4	Fulham	Prem	H	W 4-2
Sat 11	Portsmouth	Prem	A	W 3-1
Sat 18	Liverpool	FAC Rd5	A	L 0-1
Sun 26	Wigan Athletic	CC Final	N	W 4-0

February was a mix of emotions for United.
Losing a seven-goal thriller at Ewood Park was not the ideal start to the month, but consecutive league victories over Fulham and Portsmouth, both of which included Ronaldo doubles, got United back to winning ways.

The last two games of the month were bittersweet. First came the bitter part, as the Reds' hopes of making a second cup final were ended with defeat at Anfield in the FA Cup. The sight of Alan Smith being carried off the pitch with a dislocated ankle and broken left leg completed a miserable day and brought the midfielder's season to an early end. But the month finished on a sweet note as Gary Neville led United to the team's first piece of silverware as captain. The Carling Cup final victory over Wigan was never in doubt after Wayne Rooney gave the Reds a deserved lead just after the half-hour mark. He struck again on

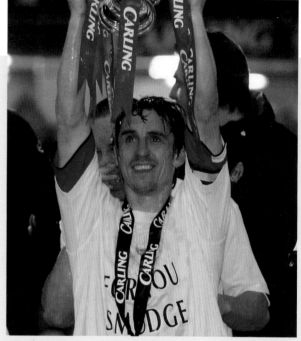

Gary Neville lifts the Carling Cup trophy at the Millennium Stadium, his first piece of silverware as club captain.

63 minutes following earlier second-half strikes from Saha and Ronaldo. The team dedicated the win to the injured Alan Smith, wearing T-shirts saying 'For You Smudge' as they went up to collect the trophy.

KEY STATS: in February...

1 own goal (scored by Fulham's Carlos Bocanegra)

4 goals were conceded and then scored by United in the opening two matches of the month

the attendance that saw United's 3-1 win at Portsmouth — the lowest Premiership attendance of the season for a Reds' match

20,206

8 of United's **14** goals were scored by Ruud and Ronaldo

PLAYER OF THE MONTH

Cristiano Ronaldo terrorised all those that crossed his path on his way to five goals in four games in February. The day before his 21st birthday (on 5 February) Ronaldo produced two treats of his own with a brace against Fulham. Two more goals followed in the victory at Portsmouth, before he rounded off the month in style with a great finish for United's third Carling Cup final goal.

MARCH 2006

Mon 6	Wigan Athletic	Prem	A	W 2-1
Sun 12	Newcastle United	Prem	H	W 2-0
Sat 18	West Bromwich Albion	Prem	A	W 2-1
Sun 26	Birmingham City	Prem	H	W 3-0
Wed 29	West Ham United	Prem	H	W 1-0

KEY STATS: in March...

GOALS	
10	**2**
scored	conceded

500 United appearances for Gary Neville

the points gap between United and Chelsea on 11 March **18**

the points gap on 29 March **9**

With the Carling Cup in the bag, United pressed on in the league. The month began with the aim of beating Liverpool to second spot and clinching automatic qualification to the Champions League. But, unlikely as it had seemed, March ended with United challenging Chelsea's grip on the title. The huge turnaround was purely down to United's fantastic form: five Premiership wins out of five, ten goals scored and just two conceded. The Carling Cup win at the end of February had played its part, filling the team with confidence.

Wayne Rooney led the way with three goals and a show of skill, strength and determination. His partnership with Louis Saha up front proved vital. Saha's pace and strength complemented Rooney's intelligent play. The French striker's 11 goals in 12 starts since returning from injury

in November kept Ruud van Nistelrooy on the bench. Rooney scored two to defeat Newcastle, while Saha struck twice to beat West Brom. Ronaldo was also in dazzling form, but it was the unlikely central-midfield partnership of Ryan Giggs and John O'Shea – ever-present in March – that offered protection to United's defence and the freedom for Rooney, Ronaldo and Saha to do the damage up front.

Wayne Rooney was in excellent form as United won all five matches in March. He struck two in the 2-0 win over Newcastle.

SIR ALEX SAID...

'I hope Chelsea are thinking about us. If they do slip up then we have to make sure we are there to take advantage. We've improved and I'm delighted with the football we're playing. We're in such good form, Chelsea know we're there behind them.'

11

APRIL 2006

Sat 1	Bolton Wanderers	Prem	A	W 2-1
Sun 9	Arsenal	Prem	H	W 2-0
Fri 14	Sunderland	Prem	H	D 0-0
Mon 17	Tottenham Hotspur	Prem	A	W 2-1
Sat 29	Chelsea	Prem	A	L 0-3

Sunderland keeper Kelvin Davies denies United again as the Reds' title hopes end with a 0-0 draw at Old Trafford.

KEY STATS: in April...

0-0
The Sunderland stalemate was one of eight goalless draws in 2005/06

GOALS

6	5
scored	conceded

150
goals for Ruud van Nistelrooy – only the eighth player in United's history to reach that figure

April 29 2006 is a date all United fans would rather forget. Not only did they have to watch Chelsea celebrate their second consecutive title after United's humiliating 3-0 defeat at Stamford Bridge, they also witnessed a cruel blow for their Player of the Year Wayne Rooney, who became the latest victim to be struck down by the curse of the metatarsal, just weeks before the World Cup.

Earlier in the month, United's slim title ambitions suffered a hammer blow against one of the poorest clubs in Premiership history. No result could have summed up the phrase 'Football's a funny old game' more than the Reds' Good Friday night stalemate with bottom-of-the-table Sunderland at Old Trafford. In Kelvin Davies, United came up against a goalkeeper in inspired form; indeed he stopped virtually everything that came his way from the feet of van Nistelrooy and Ronaldo in particular. But it was a game the Reds should have won especially as it came on the back of nine straight wins. Just over 12 hours later Chelsea took full advantage during their trip to Bolton and stretched their lead to nine points.

United did their best to keep the race alive for another two weeks with a 2-1 win at Tottenham, but it wasn't to be as José Mourinho's men kept a firm grip on their Championship crown.

HIGHS AND LOWS FOR ROONEY

It was a bittersweet month for Wayne Rooney. After firing three goals in as many games in the victories over Arsenal and Tottenham, the striker was honoured by his fellow professionals and named the PFA's Young Player of the Year for the second consecutive year. But his world came crashing down when he broke a bone in his foot at Stamford Bridge just weeks before the start of the World Cup.

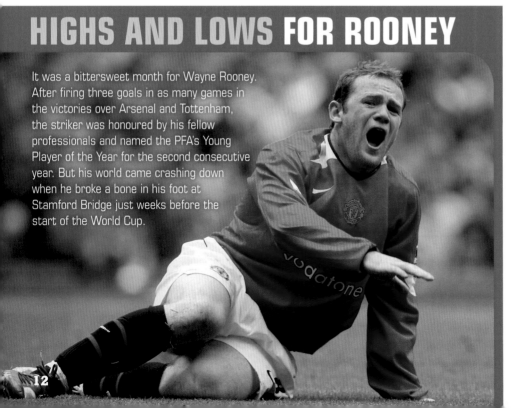

12

MAY 2006

Mon 1	Middlesbrough	Prem	H	D 0-0
Sun 7	Charlton Athletic	Prem	H	W 4-0

Patrice Evra wins the ball in his eighth start of the season, but United are held 0-0 by Boro.

The disappointment of seeing Chelsea clinch the league title in front of their own fans was followed by a frustrating stalemate at Old Trafford against Middlesbrough. It was United's fifth league draw of the season at Old Trafford. Interestingly, the Reds' away form in 2005/06 was better than Chelsea's. United picked up 39 points on the road, three more than José Mourinho's side. But it was United's inconsistent home form that ensured the Premiership trophy stayed at Stamford Bridge. Chelsea dropped just two points at home all season, compared to United's 13. The 0-0 draw with Middlesbrough left the Reds needing victory against Charlton to fend off Liverpool's challenge for second place and the automatic Champions League qualifying spot.

Sir Alex's side responded brilliantly to the task, smashing four past Charlton, whose manager Alan Curbishley was 'celebrating' his last game in charge. The win was overshadowed by the absence of Ruud van Nistelrooy, who wasn't included in the squad. Even without the Dutchman, the Reds didn't struggle for goals. Saha, Ronaldo, an own goal from Jason Euell and a wonderful strike from Richardson secured the 4-0 victory. The result ended the season on a positive note and left fans hoping for more of the same in 2006/07.

HOT SHOT

Kieran Richardson wins the ball on the halfway line and charges towards goal in the 58th minute. Moving within shooting distance, he smashes a low shot from 30 yards into the bottom corner, his sixth goal of the season.

KEY STATS: in May...

72 League goals scored after 4-0 win over Charlton	
27 clean sheets in 2005/06	
attendance against Charlton	**73,006**
8 points gap between United and Chelsea	
points dropped at Old Trafford in 2005/06	**13**

23

CARLING CUP
THE ROAD TO CARDIFF

UNITED HAVE OFTEN USED THE LEAGUE CUP TO GIVE FIRST-TEAM CHANCES TO YOUNG PLAYERS, SO MUCH SO THEY HAVE BEEN CRITICISED FOR SUPPOSEDLY NOT TAKING THE TOURNAMENT SERIOUSLY. BUT, IN 2005/06, SIR ALEX FERGUSON PROVED BOTH CAN BE ACHIEVED AS UNITED EMBARKED ON THE ROAD TO CARDIFF AND THE LEAGUE CUP FINAL...

THIRD ROUND

MANCHESTER UNITED 4
BARNET 1
Old Trafford, Wednesday 26 October 2005
A young United side got off to the perfect start in the competition, with goals from Liam Miller, Kieran Richardson, Giuseppe Rossi and Sylvan Ebanks-Blake. Debuts were given to Lee Martin, Ritchie Jones, Adam Eckersley and Darron Gibson, while Gerard Pique, Rossi and Ebanks-Blake were handed their first starts of the season. All in all, it was a successful run-out for the youngsters and a good result for the Reds.

Young Italian striker Giuseppe Rossi celebrates after scoring United's third goal against Barnet.

FOURTH ROUND

MANCHESTER UNITED 3
WEST BROMWICH ALBION 1
Old Trafford, Wednesday 30 November 2005
Goals from John O'Shea, Cristiano Ronaldo and Louis Saha gave United an impressive victory against Bryan Robson's men. But this match will be remembered as a tribute to George Best, who had passed away five days previously. Old Trafford was a sea of pictures of the late, great former United and Northern Ireland winger. The minute's silence was emotional and fans chanted his name throughout the match which had goals and attacking football. It was the perfect tribute to one of football's greatest ever players.

QUARTER-FINAL

BIRMINGHAM CITY 1
MANCHESTER UNITED 3
St Andrews, Tuesday 20 December 2005
The Reds travelled to St Andrews in the middle of a hectic fixture schedule in December. This match was one of nine matches in four weeks for Sir Alex's side. Louis Saha, finding his form after a lengthy injury spell, scored twice in what would be the start of a run of 10 goals in 10 starts for the Frenchman. Ji-sung Park got the other goal, his first strike for the club, a brilliant long-range drive.

Louis Saha fires an unstoppable half volley during United's quarter-final victory at Birmingham. It was his second goal of the match and the Reds' third.

SEMI-FINAL, FIRST LEG

BLACKBURN ROVERS 1
MANCHESTER UNITED 1
Ewood Park, Wednesday 11 January 2006

United's run to the semi-finals had been relatively straightforward. But a two-legged last-four tie with Mark Hughes' Blackburn side would be anything but easy. In a tough battle, the Reds fought for the lead when Louis Saha scored his fourth goal in three Carling Cup matches 15 minutes before the break. However, Morten Gamst Pedersen equalised for Rovers five minutes later. It ended 1-1, setting up a tense second leg at Old Trafford two weeks later.

Sir Alex Ferguson, his assistant Carlos Queiroz and Blackburn boss Mark Hughes watch from the touchline during the Carling Cup semi-final first leg at Ewood Park.

SEMI-FINAL, SECOND LEG

MANCHESTER UNITED 2
BLACKBURN ROVERS 1
Old Trafford, Wednesday 25 January 2006

With a place in the final at stake, United brought in the big guns with Ruud van Nistelrooy starting his first match of the competition alongside Wayne Rooney. Experience was needed and it paid off. Van Nistelrooy put the Reds in front before Steven Reid equalised. The Dutch striker then saw his spot-kick saved by Blackburn keeper Brad Friedel just before half-time. But Louis Saha scored his fifth goal in the competition in the second half, securing a 3-2 aggregate win and a place in the final at the Millennium Stadium.

2005/06 CARLING CUP GOALSCORERS

Louis Saha 6 in 5 games
Wayne Rooney 2 in 4 games
Cristiano Ronaldo 2 in 4 games
Sylvan Ebanks-Blake 1 in 1 game
Liam Miller 1 in 1 game
Ruud van Nistelrooy 1 in 2 games
Ji-sung Park 1 in 3 games
Giuseppe Rossi 1 in 3 games
John O'Shea 1 in 4 games
Kieran Richardson 1 in 5 games
Total goals scored 17

15

CARLING CUP
THE FINAL

THE CARLING CUP MAY HAVE BEEN UNITED'S ONLY TROPHY IN 2005/06, BUT THE FINAL WAS A GOOD DAY OUT FOR THE FANS AND THE CHANCE FOR A HOST OF REDS TO EARN THEIR FIRST WINNERS' MEDAL WITH THE CLUB. HERE'S THE STORY OF THE DAY IN PICTURES...

 33 MINS

Wayne Rooney breaks clear of Wigan's defence before sidefooting in the opening goal to give the Reds a half-time lead.

33 MINS

 55 MINS

Louis Saha taps home United's second. Rooney is first to congratulate the Frenchman on scoring his sixth goal in the competition.

55 MINS

59 MINS

 59 MINS

Four minutes later, Ronaldo celebrates having scored United's third. He pulls off his shirt and runs towards the United fans.

 61 MINS

Rooney scores his second and United's fourth with a close-range tap-in, earning him the Man of the Match award.

'IT WAS DESPERATELY IMPORTANT THAT WE WON A TROPHY AFTER THE CRITICISM WE'VE TAKEN OVER THE LAST YEAR OR SO. I HOPE THIS IS THE START OF SOMETHING SPECIAL FOR US.'
GARY NEVILLE

'THIS HAS GIVEN THOSE PLAYERS WHO HAVEN'T WON ANYTHING BEFORE A TASTE OF WHAT IT TAKES AND WHAT IT FEELS LIKE TO WIN A TROPHY AND HOPEFULLY THEY'LL WANT THAT TASTE AGAIN AND AGAIN.'
RYAN GIGGS

'IT WAS GREAT TO SEE ALL THE FANS CELEBRATING AROUND THE STADIUM. I WAS DELIGHTED TO SCORE TWO GOALS AND HOPEFULLY THIS IS THE FIRST OF MANY MORE MEDALS FOR ME WITH UNITED.'
WAYNE ROONEY

Statistics 2005/06

Rio Ferdinand congratulates Louis Saha after the Reds striker scored against Charlton Athletic in the last game of the season.

AUGUST 2005

Tue 9	CL QR3	DEBRECENI	W 3-0	Ronaldo, Rooney, van Nistelrooy
Sat 13	Prem	Everton	W 2-0	Rooney, van Nistelrooy
Sat 20	Prem	ASTON VILLA	W 1-0	van Nistelrooy
Wed 24	CL QR3	Debreceni	W 3-0	Heinze (2), Richardson
Sun 28	Prem	Newcastle United	W 2-0	Rooney, van Nistelrooy

SEPTEMBER 2005

Sat 10	Prem	MANCHESTER CITY	D 1-1	van Nistelrooy
Wed 14	CL GpD	Villarreal	D 0-0	
Sun 18	Prem	Liverpool	D 0-0	
Sat 24	Prem	BLACKBURN ROVERS	L 1-2	van Nistelrooy
Tue 27	CL GpD	BENFICA	W 2-1	Giggs, van Nistelrooy

OCTOBER 2005

Sat 1	Prem	Fulham	W 3-2	Rooney, van Nistelrooy (2)
Sat 15	Prem	Sunderland	W 3-1	Rooney, van Nistelrooy, Rossi
Tues 18	CL GpD	LILLE	D 0-0	
Sat 22	Prem	TOTTENHAM HOTSPUR	D 1-1	Silvestre
Wed 26	CC Rd3	BARNET	W 4-1	Miller, Richardson, Rossi, Ebanks-Blake
Sat 29	Prem	Middlesbrough	L 1-4	Ronaldo

NOVEMBER 2005

Wed 2	CL GpD	Lille	L 0-1	
Sun 6	Prem	CHELSEA	W 1-0	Fletcher
Sat 19	Prem	Charlton Athletic	W 3-1	Smith, van Nistelrooy (2)
Tue 22	CL GpD	VILLARREAL	D 0-0	
Sun 27	Prem	West Ham United	W 2-1	O'Shea, Rooney
Wed 30	CC Rd4	WEST BROMWICH ALBION	W 3-1	O'Shea, Ronaldo, Saha

DECEMBER 2005

Sat 3	Prem	PORTSMOUTH	W 3-0	Scholes, Rooney, van Nistelrooy
Wed 7	CL GpD	Benfica	L 1-2	Scholes
Sun 11	Prem	EVERTON	D 1-1	Giggs
Wed 14	Prem	WIGAN ATHLETIC	W 4-0	Ferdinand, Rooney (2), van Nistelrooy
Sat 17	Prem	Aston Villa	W 2-0	Rooney, van Nistelrooy
Tue 20	CC QF	Birmingham City	W 3-1	Park, Saha (2)
Mon 26	Prem	WEST BROMWICH ALBION	W 3-0	Ferdinand, Scholes, van Nistelrooy
Wed 28	Prem	Birmingham City	D 2-2	Rooney, van Nistelrooy
Sat 31	Prem	BOLTON WANDERERS	W 4-1	Ronaldo (2), Saha, N'Gotty (og)

Edwin van der Sar celebrates keeping another clean sheet as United beat Chelsea 1-0 at Old Trafford in November.

JANUARY 2006

Tue 3	Prem	Arsenal	D 0-0	
Sun 8	FAC Rd3	Burton Albion	D 0-0	
Wed 11	CC SF/1L	Blackburn Rovers	D 1-1	Saha
Sat 14	Prem	Manchester City	L 1-3	van Nistelrooy
Wed 18	FAC Rd3/R	BURTON ALBION	W 5-0	Richardson, Rossi (2), Saha, Giggs
Sun 22	Prem	LIVERPOOL	W 1-0	Ferdinand
Wed 25	CC SF/2L	BLACKBURN ROVERS	W 2-1	Saha, van Nistelrooy
Sun 29	FAC Rd4	Wolverhampton Wanderers	W 3-0	Richardson (2), Saha

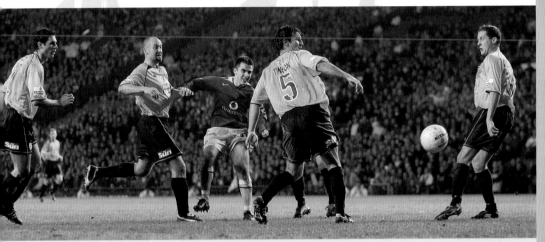

Giuseppe Rossi scored two goals during the FA Cup Third Round replay against Burton Albion on 18 January 2006. The 5-0 victory was United's biggest win of the season.

FEBRUARY 2006

Wed 1	Prem	Blackburn Rovers	L 3-4	Saha, van Nistelrooy (2)
Sat 4	Prem	FULHAM	W 4-2	Ronaldo (2), Saha, Bocanegra (og)
Sat 11	Prem	Portsmouth	W 3-1	Ronaldo (2), van Nistelrooy
Sat 18	FAC Rd5	Liverpool	L 0-1	
Sun 26	CC Final	Wigan Athletic	W 4-0	Rooney (2), Ronaldo, Saha

MARCH 2006

Mon 6	Prem	Wigan Athletic	W 2-1	Ronaldo, Chimbonda (og)
Sun 12	Prem	NEWCASTLE UNITED	W 2-0	Rooney (2)
Sat 18	Prem	West Bromwich Albion	W 2-1	Saha (2)
Sun 26	Prem	BIRMINGHAM CITY	W 3-0	Taylor (og), Giggs, Rooney
Wed 29	Prem	WEST HAM UNITED	W 1-0	van Nistelrooy

APRIL 2006

Sat 1	Prem	Bolton Wanderers	W 2-1	Saha, van Nistelrooy
Sun 9	Prem	ARSENAL	W 2-0	Park, Rooney
Fri 14	Prem	SUNDERLAND	D 0-0	
Mon 17	Prem	Tottenham Hotspur	W 2-1	Rooney (2)
Sat 29	Prem	Chelsea	L 0-3	

MAY 2006

Mon 1	Prem	MIDDLESBROUGH	D 0-0	
Sun 7	Prem	CHARLTON ATHLETIC	W 4-0	Saha, Ronaldo, Euell (og), Richardson

Ruud van Nistelrooy, who was United's highest goalscorer in 2005/06, scores from the penalty spot, the fourth goal in the Reds' 4-0 Premiership win over Wigan at Old Trafford in December.

FACTS AND FIGURES

Total matches played 56
Premiership 38
Champions League 8
Carling Cup 6
FA Cup 4

TOP FIVE APPEARANCE MAKERS
Rio Ferdinand 52 (50 starts)
Edwin van der Sar 51 (51 starts)
Wayne Rooney 48 (44 starts)
Mikael Silvestre 48 (44 starts)
John O'Shea 47 (46 starts)

TOP FIVE GOALSCORERS
Ruud van Nistelrooy 24
Wayne Rooney 19
Louis Saha 15
Cristiano Ronaldo 12
Kieran Richardson 6

Total goals scored 106
Total goals conceded 44
Clean sheets 27

Highest attendance
73,006 (v Charlton)
Biggest win
5-0 v Burton Albion (FA Cup)
Heaviest defeat
1-4 v Middlesbrough (Premiership)
Most goals in a game
7 (3-4 v Blackburn, Premiership)
Penalties for 3
Penalties against 2
Own goals 4
Longest winning sequence
9 games

Treble Triumph

In the summer of 2006, Rene Meulensteen became manager of Danish side Brondby. It was a big loss for United after he led the Reserves to the Treble. In his own words, Rene relives an unforgettable final campaign...

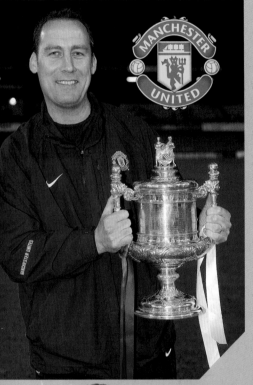

FA PREMIER RESERVE LEAGUE

'Managing the Reserves is like a juggling act. There are three groups of players you need to think about. You have your regular core players – during the 2005/06 campaign they were Giuseppe Rossi, Gerard Pique and Markus Neumayr, who were all instrumental in winning the Treble. Then there are the first team members who need a game to aid their recovery from injury. Finally, you have the promising youngsters that come up from the Academy. I fielded over 50 players last season but, no matter who was involved, we always maintained our attacking style of play.

'The game with then league leaders Middlesbrough – my first match in charge – in October 2005 was crucial because our 2-1 victory put us level on points with them. And the back-to-back wins over West Brom and Manchester City a few weeks before Easter were vital as it gave the whole squad the belief and confidence to go on and win the title. The 1-0 victory away at Villa, which sealed it for us, was an excellent display as well. Hopefully the team will win many more League championships in years to come.'

FINAL FA PREMIER RESERVE LEAGUE TABLE (Top 5 Teams)

	P	W	D	L	F	A	GD	Pts
MANCHESTER UNITED	28	19	2	7	68	32	+36	59
Aston Villa	28	16	8	4	59	26	+33	56
Manchester City	28	15	8	5	47	37	+10	53
Middlesbrough	28	15	7	6	50	27	+23	52
Newcastle United	28	12	8	8	45	40	+5	44

Fraizer Campbell (far right) celebrates scoring the winning goal against Aston Villa that clinched the title.

RESERVE PLAYER OF THE YEAR 2005/06

GIUSEPPE ROSSI

After firing 30 goals in all competitions for the Reserves, including 26 in 25 league appearances, Giuseppe was deservedly recognised by ManUtd.com readers who voted him their star man.

MANCHESTER SENIOR CUP FINAL

OLDHAM ATHLETIC 2 Wolfenden (60), Hall (72)
MANCHESTER UNITED 3 Rossi (20), Campbell (36 & 43)
Boundary Park, 25 April 2006

'This game was a tale of two halves. Before kick-off I told the players they must treat every cup final with equal respect because if you don't treat smaller finals with the same respect as the bigger occasions, you'll never win the top trophies. Mental toughness is very important in these situations – you have to keep your focus on the performance. To help the players do that I set them targets and in the first half they achieved those targets which pleased me. We gave away two sloppy goals after the break and created problems for ourselves. But, the most positive aspect of the night was that we held on and won the Cup.'

United's jubilant Reserves pose with the Cup after the victory over Oldham.

KEY STATS

- ☺ **68 goals** were scored by United in the league
- ☺ **12 games** where the Reds scored four or more goals
- ☺ **42 goals** scored by Giuseppe Rossi and Fraizer Campbell
- ☺ **3 own goals** in United's favour
- ☺ **56 players** in total turned out for the Reserves
- ☺ **19** of those players scored

FA PREMIER RESERVE LEAGUE PLAY-OFF SHIELD

MANCHESTER UNITED 2 Pique (27), Solskjaer (29)
TOTTENHAM HOTSPUR 0
Old Trafford, 4 May 2006

'This was the icing on the cake. Throughout the season I always felt the team were in the right frame of mind when it really mattered in key games and this was a good example of that. In the latter stages of the season I drew three boxes representing the League, the Senior Cup and the Play-off Shield with a 'yes/no' option under each one on a flipchart at the training ground. After winning each trophy I got the players to tick the relevant boxes. By the end of the season every one of the 'yes' boxes had been checked which gave the whole squad a real sense of fulfilment. Completing the Treble was a fantastic achievement, one I am very proud of.'

Markus Neumayr lifts the Barclays Premiership Reserve League Play-off Shield.

Edwin van der Sar

Goalkeepers

BORN **29 OCTOBER 1970, VOORHOUT, HOLLAND**
SIGNED **1 JULY 2005, FROM FULHAM**
OTHER CLUBS **AJAX, JUVENTUS**
UNITED DEBUT **9 AUGUST 2005 v DEBRECENI (H)**
CHAMPIONS LEAGUE
INTERNATIONAL TEAM **HOLLAND**

Sir Alex Ferguson wanted Edwin van der Sar, then at Ajax, after Peter Schmeichel left Old Trafford at the end of the Treble-winning season in 1999. But the Dutchman had also attracted Europe's other top clubs, and eventually joined Juventus in 2001. However, after two years, the Italian giants signed Gianluigi Buffon for £33million from Parma and Edwin was transferred to Fulham for £5million. Six years after targeting van der Sar, Sir Alex finally got his man in summer 2005. Schmeichel clearly approved. 'Edwin has everything,' he said. 'He always performs at the highest level.' In Edwin's debut season at Old Trafford, he kept 25 clean sheets and won his first trophy in England as the Reds beat Wigan in the Carling Cup final. 'I was pleased with my first season,' he said. 'But there's room for improvement. Our Champions League exit at the Group Stage was disappointing. We're determined to do better next season.'

CAREER HISTORY

Years	Club	Appearances	Goals
1992–1999	Ajax	226	1
1999–2001	Juventus	66	0
2001–2005	Fulham	127	0
2005–present	Manchester United	38	0

CAREER HONOURS

Dutch League **1994, 1995, 1996, 1998**
Dutch Cup **1993, 1998, 1999**
English League Cup **2006**
Champions League **1995**
European Super Cup **1995**
Inter-Continental Cup **1995**

DID YOU KNOW?

It's Edwin's job to stop goals going in, but he has proved he can score them, too. While playing for Ajax in 1997/98, Edwin scored a penalty to complete a 9-1 victory over De Graaftshap.

Tim Howard

- **Born** 6 March 1979, New Jersey, USA
- **Signed** 15 July 2003, from Metrostars
- **Fee** £2.3million
- **Other Clubs** None
- **United Debut** 10 August 2003 v Arsenal (N) Community Shield
- **International Team** USA

In the summer of 2005, the departure of Roy Carroll appeared to have opened the way for Tim Howard to claim the No.1 spot at Old Trafford. However, Edwin van der Sar's arrival from Fulham saw the American keeper spend much of the season on the bench – he made only five starts in 2005/06. But, aged 26, he is young for a goalkeeper. His peak years are still ahead of him, as van der Sar points out. 'Tim has good qualities,' the Dutchman said. 'He is learning all the time. All the goalkeepers want to play all the games, but Tim is still only young so I think he has a good future ahead of him.' After competing in the 2006 World Cup finals for the USA, Tim returned to England, but not with United. Before the tournament he agreed a loan move to Everton for the 2006/07 campaign.

Tim Howard became the first ever American to play for United when the New Jersey-born goalkeeper joined the Reds in 2003.

Ben Foster

- **Born** 3 April 1983, Leamington Spa
- **Signed** 19 July 2005, from Stoke City
- **Fee** £1million
- **Other Clubs** Racing Club Warwick, Wrexham (loan), Watford (loan)
- **International Team** England

Ben Foster was spotted by United while on loan from Stoke to Wrexham. Sir Alex Ferguson was watching his son, Darren, playing in the LDV Vans Trophy final in 2005, which saw Wrexham beat Southend United.

Ben Foster's fairytale £1million move to Old Trafford from Championship side Stoke City in July 2005, continued his rapid rise up the football ladder. He joined Stoke's academy from non-league Racing Club Warwick in August 2002. Although he was highly rated and stood out in Stoke's youth and reserve sides, he never played a first team match at the Britannia Stadium. Foster was soon loaned to Championship side Watford, where he earned a regular first team place and helped the Hornets gain promotion to the Premiership through the play-offs in May 2006. Shortly after Watford beat Leeds 3-0 in the play-off final, Ben was called-up as a reserve for England's 2006 World Cup squad. Although he wasn't included in the final squad it was further proof of his dramatic development. He is likely to spend much of the 2006/07 season gaining valuable experience as Edwin van der Sar's understudy.

Gary Neville
Full backs

MANCHESTER UNITED

BORN **18 FEBRUARY 1975, BURY**
SIGNED **8 JULY 1991, TRAINEE**
OTHER CLUBS **NONE**
UNITED DEBUT **16 SEPTEMBER 1992 v TORPEDO MOSCOW (H), UEFA CUP**
INTERNATIONAL TEAM **ENGLAND**

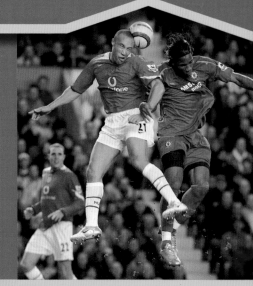

The 2005/06 season was one of mixed fortunes for United die-hard Gary Neville. It began on a sour note when a groin injury he suffered in the 3-0 victory away to Debreceni put him out of action for three months. He returned to the starting line-up in the Carling Cup win over West Brom in November and was a virtual ever-present for the remainder of the season. Neville was handed what he describes as 'the highest honour I've ever been given' when he was made club captain following Roy Keane's departure. From the outset he said he wanted to be remembered as a leader that helped United win trophies. He got off to the perfect start, skippering the Reds to a 4-0 Carling Cup final win over Wigan in February 2006. A month later, he celebrated his 500th game in a red shirt in United's 3-0 victory over Birmingham.

DID YOU KNOW?

Gary Neville was the eighth player to reach 500 appearances for United. Sir Bobby Charlton, Bill Foulkes, Ryan Giggs, Alex Stepney, Tony Dunne, Denis Irwin and Joe Spence are the others.

Mikael was part of the Inter Milan side beaten in the Champions League quarter-final in March 1999 on the way to United's Treble triumph.

GARY'S FIVE BEST MOMENTS

16 September 1992 United 0-0 Torpedo Moscow (UEFA Cup)
'My debut is the proudest moment of my career. I got a taste of things that night and knew I wanted to do it again and again.'
5 May 1997 United 3-3 Middlesbrough (Premiership)
'The ball came to me and I remember thinking "just hit it true and sweet". Thankfully I did that and scored my first United goal.'
21 April 1999 Juventus 2-3 United (Champions League)
'To go to Juventus, who had haunted us for four or five years previously, and come back from two goals down was incredible.'
26 May 1999 Bayern Munich 1-2 United (Champions League)
'It doesn't get any better than winning the European Cup with your brother and your best mates – one of the greatest nights of my life.'
26 February 2006 United 4-0 Wigan (Carling Cup)
'Lifting the Carling Cup as captain was a great moment and I hope that trophy will be the first of many.'

Mikael Silvestre

- Born 9 August 1977, Chambray-Les-Tours, France
- Signed 10 September 1999, from Inter Milan
- Fee £4million
- Other Clubs Rennes
- United Debut 11 September 1999 v Liverpool (A) Premiership
- International Team France

Since joining United in September 1999, Mikael has enjoyed prolonged spells at both centre-back and left-back. Aside from his defensive qualities, the versatile Frenchman, who was part of France's 2006 World Cup squad, has also proved himself to be just as effective at the other end. United fans will remember his brace in the 2-1 victory over Liverpool in September 2004 and he also has the ability to deliver dangerous crosses, as he proved in the 2-0 victory over Arsenal in April 2006. Mikael's pinpoint crossfield ball fell straight at the feet of Wayne Rooney, who blasted home United's first goal. A quick and steady defender, Silvestre has now made well over 300 appearances for the Reds despite stiff competition for places in the back four. The contest for places almost prompted him to swap United for French champions Olympique Lyonnais during the 2006 January transfer window. However, he rejected Lyon's offer, insisting his future was with the Reds.

Phil Bardsley

- Born 28 June 1985, Salford
- Signed 1 July 2001, trainee
- Other Clubs Burnley (loan)
- United Debut 3 December 2003 v West Brom (A) Carling Cup

The 2005/06 season was a breakthrough campaign for 'Bardo'. He made his first start for the club – a Man of the Match display in the 2-1 win over Benfica in September 2005 – then enjoyed his longest spell in the side. Filling in for the injured Gary Neville at right-back, Phil started five of United's next six games, and only lost his place when Neville returned. He was loaned to Burnley for two months at the end of the season to gain further first team experience.

Phil has been at Old Trafford since he was eight, working his way up through the club's ranks.

Gerard's surname is Bernabeu, the same name as Real Madrid's ground. His grandfather, Amador Bernabeu, was vice-President of FC Barcelona.

Gerard Pique

- Born 2 February 1987, Barcelona, Spain
- Signed 1 October 2004, trainee
- Other Clubs Barcelona
- United Debut 26 October 2004 v Crewe Alexandra (A) Carling Cup

Gerard Pique is another promising young defender, signed from Barcelona in the summer 2004. Highly regarded at the Nou Camp, Pique moved to Manchester to benefit from United's famed youth system. 'I'll give everything I have got,' Pique promised on his arrival. He made his senior debut almost immediately, as a substitute in the Carling Cup against Crewe in October 2004. Crucial in the Reserves' Treble last season, he has a bright future. Expect to see more of this talented central defender in the coming years.

Gabriel Heinze

Full backs

BORN **19 APRIL 1978, CRESPO, ARGENTINA**
SIGNED **11 JUNE 2004, FROM PARIS SAINT GERMAIN**
FEE **£6.9MILLION**
OTHER CLUBS **NEWELL'S OLD BOYS, REAL VALLADOLID**
UNITED DEBUT **11 SEPTEMBER 2004 v BOLTON (A) PREMIERSHIP**
INTERNATIONAL TEAM **ARGENTINA**

Gabriel Heinze has experienced mixed fortunes during his two-year spell at Old Trafford. He missed the opening month of his first season due to his involvement in the Olympic Games with Argentina, where he won a gold medal. On his arrival in Manchester, the left-back scored just 44 minutes into his debut at Bolton in September 2004. His determined and committed approach quickly made him a favourite with United fans and he capped off his first year by claiming the Sir Matt Busby Player of the Year award. He began the 2005/06 campaign in excellent form, scoring twice against Debreceni in the Champions League. However, three weeks later his season was over when he injured his knee in the European clash with Villarreal. Hard work and sheer determination earned him a place in Argentina's World Cup squad. His United return was eagerly anticipated – a sign of how important he has become to the Reds.

DID YOU KNOW?

During his time at PSG, Heinze was voted the toughest defender in French football by readers of one of France's best-read newspapers.

GABBY'S HIGHS AND LOWS

UP September 2004 Scores on his United debut.
DOWN April 2005 Sustains ankle injury which forces him to miss FA Cup final.
UP July 2005 Becomes the first ever defender to be voted Sir Matt Busby Player of the Year.
UP August 2005 Scores twice in his first start of the season during the 3-0 win over Debreceni.

DOWN September 2005 Ruled out for the remainder of the 2005/06 campaign after damaging cruciate knee ligaments against Villarreal.
DOWN December 2005 Sir Alex says he fears Gabby will not be fit for the World Cup.
UP April 2006 Makes a surprise return to the bench for the home game with Sunderland.
UP May 2006 Named in Argentina's World Cup squad.

Patrice Evra

- **Born** 15 May 1981, Dakar, Senegal
- **Signed** 10 January 2006, from Monaco
- **Fee** Undisclosed
- **Other Clubs** Monza, Nice
- **United Debut** 14 January 2006 v Manchester City (A) Premiership
- **International Team** France

Patrice comes from a rather large family. The French defender has an incredible 23 brothers and sisters!

Patrice Evra endured a tough United debut as the Reds went down 3-1 at Manchester City after a poor team performance. Evra, who joined from Monaco just four days earlier, played 45 minutes of the disappointing encounter before being withdrawn at half-time. His next match in a red shirt came in another local derby, this time at home to Liverpool – and provided a much better outcome. He earned the free-kick which Ryan Giggs crossed for Rio Ferdinand to head the winner seconds before the final whistle. He made a dozen further appearances during the 2005/06 campaign and collected his first winners' medal with the club as a substitute in the Carling Cup final. The Frenchman will be aiming to build on his first six months at Old Trafford during the coming seasons, but knows he faces stiff competition at left-back from Gabriel Heinze and fellow countryman Mikael Silvestre.

John O'Shea

- **Born** 30 April 1981, Waterford, Ireland
- **Signed** 3 August 1998, trainee
- **Other Clubs** None
- **United Debut** 31 October 1999 v Aston Villa (A) League Cup
- **International Team** Republic of Ireland

Injured at the time, O'Shea – together with team-mates Rio Ferdinand and Phil Bardsley – sat with United's away fans at Anfield during the Reds' FA Cup fifth-round defeat to Liverpool in February 2006. He even started a chant of 'Red Army'!

Ever since first becoming a fully fledged member of the team in 2002, John O'Shea has featured in a number of different positions across the Reds' backline. But during the 2005/06 season Sir Alex Ferguson trialled the versatile Irishman in a new role in midfield. The change in position brought added responsibility but O'Shea proved he was capable of carrying the burden. Alongside Ryan Giggs, he looked solid in the holding position just in front of the back four. It was this partnership that played a crucial part in ensuring that United secured second place in the Premiership, which included automatic qualification for the Champions League, and the Carling Cup final success. He may not find himself in the same midfield role in 2006/07, but he has proved to be an extremely valuable member of the squad, always willing to play in any position for the good of the team.

Rio Ferdinand
Rio Centre backs

BORN **7 NOVEMBER 1978, LONDON**
SIGNED **22 JULY 2002, FROM LEEDS UNITED**
FEE **£30MILLION**
OTHER CLUBS **WEST HAM UNITED**
UNITED DEBUT **27 AUGUST 2003** v **ZALAEGERSZEG (H) CHAMPIONS LEAGUE**
INTERNATIONAL TEAM **ENGLAND**

FERDINAND'S FAN CLUB

'It's incredibly difficult for strikers to get past Rio. He has great strength and good leadership qualities. He's a top-class player.'
Edwin van der Sar

'He stands out because of his presence on the pitch. He stamps his authority on games with his strong personality and unique style.'
Gabriel Heinze

'Rio Ferdinand is one of the best players you will find anywhere in Europe, or even the world.'
Sven-Goran Eriksson

Rio Ferdinand signed a new contract in the summer of 2005, a welcome confirmation that the talented and cultured central defender will remain at Old Trafford for years to come. He didn't make the strongest of starts in 2005/06, but his displays quickly improved. He also ended a three-and-a-half-year wait for a United goal. It arrived in December 2005 in the 4-0 Premiership win over Wigan at Old Trafford, and a second followed two weeks later against West Brom. Ferdinand added his third in nine matches – a glorious last-gasp winner – against arch-rivals Liverpool in January. With the scores level at 0-0 as the match entered injury time, United were throwing everything at their opponents. With one last attack, Ryan Giggs fired in a free-kick from the left and Rio rose above everyone to power his header home. Old Trafford went wild. Life doesn't get much sweeter than that!

DID YOU KNOW?

Rio had a bet with his brother, West Ham's Anton Ferdinand, on who would score the most goals in 2005/06. Rio was 2-0 down until his three goals in nine games won him the bet. As a result Anton had to take his older brother out for a meal.

Wes Brown

- **Born** 13 October 1979, Manchester
- **Signed** 8 July 1996, trainee
- **Other Clubs** None
- **United Debut** 4 May 1998 v Leeds United (H) Premiership
- **International Team** England

Sir Alex once said of Wes, 'He is without question the best natural defender this club has had for years.' The United boss regularly makes that point of a defender who has made well over 200 appearances for the Reds. He's strong in the air, equally tough in the tackle, an excellent marker and quick. But, sadly, injuries have held him back. He has twice come back from serious knee injuries, and more niggling knocks interrupted his 2005/06 campaign. But he still managed 30 appearances and was expected to be included in England's World Cup squad. Sir Alex even spoke to Sven-Goran Eriksson on the phone to recommend the Manchester-born defender. It seemed ideal, with Wes having built up a solid partnership with Reds team-mate Rio Ferdinand. Although he was left out of the 23-man party, he continues to be counted as an important part of United's defence.

Nemanja Vidic

- **Born** 21 October 1981, Uzice, Yugoslavia
- **Signed** 5 January 2006, from Spartak Moscow
- **Fee** Undisclosed
- **Other Clubs** Red Star Belgrade
- **United Debut** 25 January 2006 v Blackburn (H) Carling Cup
- **International Team** Serbia & Montenegro

Wes Brown has been a professional at United for ten years. He signed pro at the age of 17, on 4 November 1996.

Nemanja Vidic turned down offers from Liverpool and Serie A side Fiorentina when he signed for the Reds in January 2006.

Nemanja Vidic was largely unknown by United fans when Sir Alex Ferguson signed him from Spartak Moscow in January 2006. Since then the tough tackling defender has earned a growing reputation among supporters. He hadn't played for six weeks when he joined the Reds – the Russian season had recently ended – so he took time to get up to speed in the Premiership. But, once he did, he looked confident and comfortable alongside Rio Ferdinand in the centre of United's defence. Injury to Wes Brown allowed Vidic – or 'Vida' as he is known to his team-mates – a chance in the side. His performances were so impressive, particularly in the 2-0 win over Arsenal in April 2006, that he managed to keep Wes out of the team. An exciting first few months have promised much to come from Vida.

Cristiano Winners Ronaldo

BORN **5 FEBRUARY 1985, MADEIRA, PORTUGAL**
SIGNED **12 AUGUST 2003, FROM SPORTING LISBON**
FEE **£12.24MILLION**
OTHER CLUBS **NONE**
UNITED DEBUT **16 AUGUST 2003 v BOLTON (H) PREMIERSHIP**
INTERNATIONAL TEAM **PORTUGAL**

HONOUR ROLL

Despite his young age, Ronaldo has racked up an impressive list of personal and team honours:

Portugal Young Sports Personality of the Year (2002)
FA Cup winner (2004)
Euro 2004 runner-up (2004)
UEFA Team of the Year (2004)
FA Cup runner-up (2005)
FIFPro Young Player of the Year (2005)
Carling Cup winner (2006)
PFA Team of the Year (2006)
United Goal of the Season (2006)

DID YOU KNOW?

His full name is Cristiano Ronaldo dos Santos Aveiro. His parents chose the name Ronaldo in honour of former US president Ronald Reagan, who was his father's favourite actor.

Cristiano Ronaldo is exciting to watch. He's full of tricks, flicks and skills that leave defenders – and often supporters – wondering how he did it. By then he has used his lightning-fast pace to get away from the defender and unleashed a powerful shot on goal. This is his fourth season at United, having joined for £12.24million from Sporting Lisbon in 2003. Vital for Portugal in the 2006 World Cup, he is as important for his country as Wayne Rooney is for England. Alongside Rooney at United, they represent the future at Old Trafford. He is sometimes criticised for his crossing or for using his tricks too often. But Ronaldo is like any young player – he is still developing. He's confident he will fulfil his potential. 'In three years' time, I want to be one of the best players in the world,'

Ji-sung Park

- **Born** 25 February 1981, Seoul, South Korea
- **Signed** 8 July 2005, from PSV Eindhoven
- **Fee** £4million
- **Other Clubs** Kyoto Purple Sanga
- **United Debut** 9 August 2005 v Debreceni (H) Champions League
- **International Team** South Korea

'I don't know what it is he's been eating, but I'd like some of it,' said Sir Alex of Ji-sung Park, or 'Ji' as he is known to his team-mates. The Reds boss was referring to the South Korean midfielder's incredible energy levels. Signed from PSV Eindhoven in July 2005, the tricky winger, who can play on either flank or in the centre of midfield, has quickly become a fans' favourite because of his skilful and committed performances. When the Reds beat Arsenal 2-0 at Old Trafford in April 2006, Park was crucial in the victory and not just because he scored United's second goal. 'Arsenal couldn't live with his energy and the runs he made in behind their defence,' said Sir Alex afterwards. Ji, who turns 26 in February 2007, made 46 appearances in his debut season with the club. He could become a very important player for the Reds in the future.

Ji-sung Park had made over 50 appearances for South Korea before his 24th birthday.

Kieran Richardson

- **Born** 21 October 1984, Greenwich
- **Signed** 2 July 2001, trainee
- **Other Clubs** West Ham United, West Bromwich Albion (loan)
- **United Debut** 23 October 2002 v Olympiakos (A) Champions League
- **International Team** England

A product of United's successful Academy youth system, Kieran made his Reds debut in 2002 in the Champions League, aged just 18. Despite his early opportunities in the first team, his chances were limited as competition for places was fierce. By August 2005 – three years after his debut – he had made only ten starts for United. Richardson's real break didn't come until, like David Beckham, a successful loan spell away from the club earned him recognition. Kieran joined West Bromwich Albion for four months at the end of the 2004/05 season and was magnificent in helping the Midlands club avoid relegation. As Sir Alex put it, the move helped him grow up. 'Kieran went to West Brom a boy, but came back a man,' he said. A good passer, quick and able to score goals, he is a valuable squad member.

Kieran Richardson was a trainee with West Ham before moving north to Manchester to join United as an Academy trainee.

Ryan Giggs

Midfielders

BORN **29 NOVEMBER 1973, CARDIFF, WALES**
SIGNED **9 JULY 1990, TRAINEE**
OTHER CLUBS **NONE**
UNITED DEBUT **2 MARCH 1991 v EVERTON (H) DIVISION ONE**
INTERNATIONAL TEAM **WALES**

Ryan Giggs was given a new lease of life in the centre of midfield during the 2005/06 season. Despite being one of the oldest players in the squad, the Welshman showed no signs of ageing limbs. Following the departure of Roy Keane and injury-enforced absence of Paul Scholes, Giggs revelled in his new position and produced one of his best displays of the campaign in the dramatic 1-0 victory over Liverpool in January 2006; delivering the free-kick for Rio Ferdinand's late winner. It is credit to Giggsy's talent as a footballer and his fitness as an athlete that he is still going strong after over 15 years at the top level. A true legend, he has over 650 appearances to his name, nearly 150 goals and 22 winners' medals in a bulging trophy cabinet. Few would bet against him adding to that list before his contract is up in June 2008.

DID YOU KNOW?

Ryan is third in the list of United's all-time appearance makers with over 650 matches under his belt. To date, only Bill Foulkes and Sir Bobby Charlton have played more United games than the Welsh winger.

RYAN GIGGS' TROPHY CABINET

Ryan has won 22 winners' medals during a glorious United career:

1991/92	**UEFA Super Cup, League Cup**
1992/93	**Premiership, Charity Shield**
1993/94	**Premiership, FA Cup, Charity Shield**
1995/96	**Premiership, FA Cup, Charity Shield**
1996/97	**Premiership, Charity Shield**
1998/99	**European Cup, Premiership, FA Cup**
1999/00	**Premiership, Inter-Continental Cup**
2000/01	**Premiership**
2002/03	**Premiership, Community Shield**
2003/04	**FA Cup**
2005/06	**League Cup**

Darren Fletcher

- **Born** 1 February 1984, Edinburgh, Scotland
- **Signed** 3 July 2000, trainee
- **Other Clubs** None
- **United Debut** 12 March 2003 v FC Basel (H) Champions League
- **International Team** Scotland

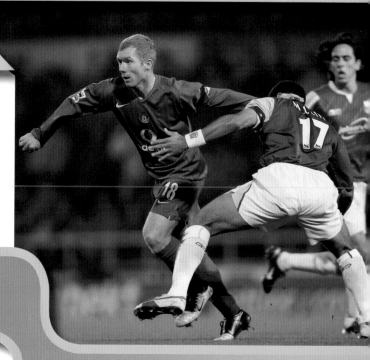

Darren's winning goal against Chelsea was his first ever at Old Trafford. His three previous goals had all come away from home.

Darren Fletcher has made rapid progress since joining United as a trainee in the summer of 2000. Not only has he become a regular in the first team squad and notched up over 100 appearances in a red shirt, he has also excelled on the international stage. He became Scotland's youngest captain for 118 years when he skippered the Tartan Army to a 1-0 friendly win over Estonia in May 2004, aged 20. A creative central midfielder, Fletcher has enjoyed prolonged spells in United's engine room during recent seasons. However, the emergence of Ryan Giggs and John O'Shea as Sir Alex Ferguson's preferred central pairing during the latter part of 2005/06 resulted in reduced opportunities for the young Scot, who also missed out on a place in the Carling Cup final squad. The highlight of his season came in November 2005 when he headed the winner against league champions Chelsea at Old Trafford.

Paul Scholes is a staunch Oldham Athletic fan and is a regular visitor to Boundary Park when he isn't on United duty.

Paul Scholes

- **Born** 16 November 1974, Salford
- **Signed** 8 July 1991, trainee
- **Other Clubs** None
- **United Debut** 24 September 1994 v Port Vale (A) League Cup
- **International Team** England

'He's a sensational player, one of the best I've ever had,' Sir Alex Ferguson says when asked about Paul Scholes. The Salford-born midfielder has been working his magic at Old Trafford for over 12 years. His creativity in the final third is matched by his unique ability to time his runs into the box. Once there he rarely misses. That was never more evident than in the 2002/03 title-winning campaign when he enjoyed arguably his finest season, netting 20 times and creating a fair share of Ruud van Nistelrooy's 44 goals. Since then, Scholes has rarely hit top form consistently. A serious eye problem forced him onto the sidelines at the halfway point of the 2005/06 campaign. But he returned as a substitute in United's final game against Charlton, and Sir Alex insists there's plenty more to come from Scholesy. 'He remains a very important player for us,' the boss says.

Wayne Rooney
Attackers

BORN **24 OCTOBER 1985, CROXTETH**
SIGNED **31 AUGUST 2004, FROM EVERTON**
FEE **UNDISCLOSED**
OTHER CLUBS **NONE**
UNITED DEBUT **28 SEPTEMBER 2004 v FENERBAHCE (H)**
CHAMPIONS LEAGUE
INTERNATIONAL TEAM **ENGLAND**

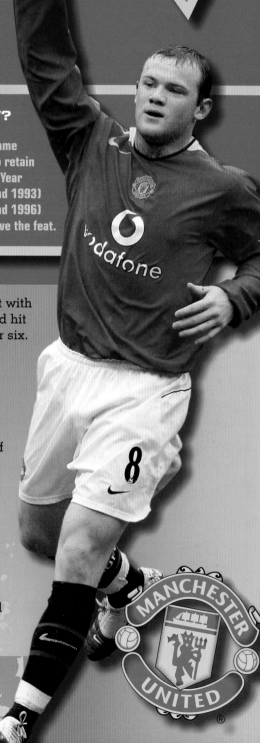

'He's the most important player in the Manchester United team,' declared Sir Alex Ferguson last season. That says it all. Goalscorer, craftsman and team talisman – the Liverpool-born striker has become one of the most influential footballers in the world. The 2005/06 campaign was Rooney's most prolific to date – 19 goals in all competitions: 16 in the Premiership, two in the League Cup final victory over Wigan and one in the Champions League – saw him improve on his debut season's total of 17. However, the campaign ended badly for Rooney when he became the latest victim of the curse of the metatarsal, breaking his foot against Chelsea in April. The injury threw England's World Cup preparations into chaos – another sign of his importance to country as well as club – but he made a speedy recovery in time to play in football's biggest competition. Proceedings ended on a sour note, however, when he was red-carded during England's quarter-final defeat to Portugal.

DID YOU KNOW?

In 2006 Wayne Rooney became only the third ever player to retain the PFA Young Player of the Year award. Ryan Giggs (1992 and 1993) and Robbie Fowler (1995 and 1996) are the only others to achieve the feat.

THE WONDER OF WAYNE

In just two seasons at Old Trafford, Rooney has provided United fans with countless memorable moments. Here are three of his best:

DEVASTATING DEBUT
United 6-2 Fenerbahce
Old Trafford, 28 September 2004
Wayne marks his Reds debut with a stunning hat-trick as United hit their European opponents for six.

NEWCASTLE NETBUSTER
United 2-1 Newcastle
Old Trafford, 24 April 2005
United are trailing 1-0, but Rooney inspires victory with an unstoppable volley, one of the best goals Old Trafford has ever seen.

DOUBLE DELIGHT
United 4-0 Wigan
Millennium Stadium,
26 February 2006
Two goals from Man of the Match Rooney helps seal a Carling Cup final victory and the striker's first winners' medal for United.

Ole Gunnar Solskjaer

- **Born** 26 February 1973, Kristiansund, Norway
- **Signed** 23 July 1996, from Molde
- **Fee** £1.5million
- **Other Clubs** Clausenengen
- **United Debut** 25 August 1996 v Blackburn (H) Premiership
- **International Team** Norway

Ole Gunnar Solskjaer is a legend in the truest sense of the term. Ole entered United history with his winning goal in the Champions League final at the Nou Camp in 1999. But his Reds career is so much more than that. Solskjaer has made over 300 United appearances and scored more than 100 goals. Popular with fans and players alike, his name was regularly sung at United games throughout a two-year absence with a serious knee injury. For his comeback match, against Birmingham City on 28 December, he was given a standing ovation. Solskjaer turns 34 in February 2007, but a new contract in March 2006 means there's life in Ole's Old Trafford playing career yet. However, even when he does hang up his boots, Solskjaer's influence at United will remain. As part of his new deal, he is gaining experience coaching United's young players.

Solskjaer cost just £1.5million from Norwegian club Molde in 1996 – that works out as little more than £130,000 a season for the 11 seasons he has been at United.

Alan Smith

- **Born** 28 October 1980, Wakefield
- **Signed** 26 May 2004, from Leeds
- **Fee** £7million
- **Other Clubs** None
- **United Debut** 8 August 2004 v Arsenal (N) Charity Shield
- **International Team** England

Alan Smith is incredibly popular at Old Trafford, with team-mates and supporters alike. A Yorkshireman admired by Mancunians isn't easy to find, but Smith has proved his commitment to United's cause, displaying a gritty determination to win. He is, without question, a fans' favourite. Usually a striker, United made use of his tackling qualities in midfield in 2005/06. Smith did well and, as you'd expect, never shirked a 50-50 challenge. However, misfortune struck against Liverpool in February 2006 when he broke his leg and dislocated his ankle. To prove his popularity at the club, when the Reds lifted the Carling Cup trophy in the following match all of United's players wore T-shirts bearing the message 'For you Smudge' in tribute to their injured team-mate. Sir Alex Ferguson praised his willpower to overcome the setback. When available, Smith is a valuable player, in midfield or attack.

Alan Smith's first sporting achievement wasn't in football. A huge fan of BMX and motocross as a kid, Smudge was crowned BMX National Champion at the age of eight.

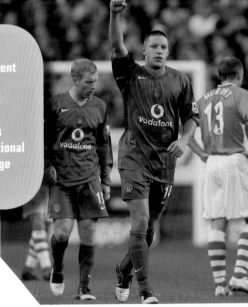

Ruud Strikers
van Nistelrooy

- BORN **1 JULY 1976, OSS, HOLLAND**
- SIGNED **23 APRIL 2001**
- FEE **£19MILLION, FROM PSV EINDHOVEN**
- OTHER CLUBS **DEN BOSCH, HEERENVEEN**
- UNITED DEBUT **12 AUGUST 2001 v LIVERPOOL (N)**
- **CHARITY SHIELD**
- INTERNATIONAL TEAM **HOLLAND**

RUUD'S 150

HOW HE SCORED THEM...
Head **20**
Right foot **113**
Left foot **17**

WHEN HE SCORED THEM...
0-15 minutes **15**
16-30 minutes **18**
31-45 minutes **32**
46-60 minutes **22**
61-75 minutes **32**
76-90 minutes **31**

THE TEAMS WORST HIT...
Goals/games
Newcastle **9** in **9**
Fulham **8** in **7**
Tottenham **7** in **9**
Charlton **8** in **6**
Everton **6** in **6**

'He's the best finisher we've ever seen at Manchester United,' says Sir Alex Ferguson when asked to describe Ruud van Nistelrooy's ability. 'There is nobody in world football that compares to him,' says his strike-partner at Old Trafford, Louis Saha. As far as natural finishers go, this Dutch goal machine is among the very finest.

In five seasons at Old Trafford, van Nistelrooy has scored an incredible 150 goals. Even more unbelievable is that he's done it in just 214 appearances. His winning goal against Bolton on 1 April 2006 saw him become only the eighth player in United's history to reach that total. It makes his £19million transfer from PSV Eindhoven in 2001, a British record fee at the time, seem like a bargain.

DID YOU KNOW?

Ruud's full name is Rutgerus Johannes Martinus van Nistelrooy. Just call him Ruud, or, if you're at a United game and he scores, 'RUUD RUUD RUUD!'

Despite scoring 24 goals in the 2005/06 season, his place in the side was by no means guaranteed as Louis Saha's goalscoring form meant the Dutchman had a serious challenger for his place in the team.

Louis Saha

- **Born** 8 August 1978, Paris, France
- **Signed** 23 January 2004, from Fulham
- **Fee** £12.82million
- **Other Clubs** Newcastle (loan), Metz
- **United Debut** 31 January 2004 v Southampton (H) Premiership
- **International Team** France

Louis Saha can hardly contain his excitement after an injury-free six months, 'It's like a miracle!' he jokes. The French striker has suffered more injury heartache than most since joining United in January 2004. But after a prolonged spell away from the treatment table and an impressive goalscoring run during the second half of the 2005/06 campaign, Louis has finally been able to display his full talents as a striker. And he's scoring plenty of goals, too. When asked to pick out his favourite strike from an ever-growing bunch, Louis immediately selects his Carling Cup final strike in the 4-0 victory over Wigan – a tap-in from three yards out. 'The best strikers have to score tap-ins,' he insists. 'I never used to score goals like that but, now that I am, I feel like a real striker.' There has been increasing evidence of that on the pitch, long may it continue.

United are Saha's third Premiership team, having played for both Fulham and Newcastle. He spent three and a half years at Craven Cottage and four and a half months on loan with the Geordies during the 1998/99 season.

Giuseppe Rossi

- **Born** 1 February 1987, New Jersey, USA
- **Signed** 6 July 2004, from Parma
- **Fee** Undisclosed
- **Other Clubs** None
- **United Debut** 10 November 2004 v Crystal Palace (H) Carling Cup

He may be the smallest member of the first team squad, but big things lie ahead for Giuseppe Rossi. He won the Reserves' Player of the Year award, netting over 30 times in the 2005/06 season. He also made his mark on the first team, scoring his first league goal just nine minutes into his Premiership debut at Sunderland. He hit the net again in the League Cup win over Barnet and fired an excellent double in the FA Cup replay win over Burton Albion. Aside from his goalscoring ability, his intelligent all-round play stands out, while he has the attitude to succeed at the highest level. Sir Alex Ferguson says the young Italian striker represents the future of the club. 'He's growing into a terrific professional with a great attitude. He's a sensational prospect,' beamed the Reds boss.

Giuseppe had the chance to play international football for either the USA or Italy. American-born, but of Italian origin, Rossi was courted by both countries, but he opted for Italy, saying it's his dream to play for the Azzurri.

ONESTOWATCH

From the Busby Babes to Fergie's Fledglings, developing young players has always been crucial at Old Trafford. Paul McGuinness, United's Under-18s coach, prepares young Reds for professional football. But it's not just talent that is required. 'Ability is vital, but character and dedication are, in many ways, the most important attributes,' Paul says. 'We help players learn and improve, but we don't make the players, the players make themselves. They have to want to succeed.' Here, McGuinness introduces five players with bright futures...

Fraizer Campbell

- Position **Striker**
- Born **13 September 1987, Huddersfield**
- Joined United as a trainee **July 2004**

'Fraizer is a very talented striker. He's very brave and has the ability to beat players and create something out of nothing. He'll challenge and chase the ball, he's a real nuisance for defenders. His athleticism and pace mean he will soon make the jump to professional football. We have to make sure players are challenged all the time. He is one that could possibly be loaned out. He will make a success of that, I am sure.'

Febian Brandy

- Position **Striker**
- Born **4 February 1989, Manchester**
- Joined United as a trainee **July 2005**

'Febian is small, but quick and powerful. Last season he returned from a broken leg, which had set him back. He has always been ahead of his age in terms of his athleticism and speed, but other players have caught up with him, so he has to develop other areas of his game and understand his position. We hope he does that. It's a challenge but he'll be up for it because he's a brave lad, a big-game player with the ability to make an impact.'

⊕ Darron Gibson

- ⊕ Position **Central midfielder**
- ⊕ Born **25 October 1987, Derry, Northern Ireland**
- ⊕ Joined United as a trainee **July 2004**

'If I had to liken Darron to another player it would be Michael Ballack. Tall and strong, he has a good range of passing and can score from distance. He came over from junior football in Ireland three years ago and since then he's made huge strides. He's one to keep an eye on, a player we hope will make the step up to league football. Darron must express himself in attack and defence, but he's constantly improving and has a big future.'

⊕ Kieran Lee

- ⊕ Position **Full-back**
- ⊕ Born **22 June 1988, Stalybridge**
- ⊕ Joined United as a trainee **July 2004**

'Kieran has a similar style to Denis Irwin; neat, tidy and efficient on the ball. He's quietly determined and I was impressed with his step up to the Reserves. He was rewarded with a contract and played in Roy Keane's testimonial. He had one tackle in that match which was close to the mark, but Kieran was determined not to be beaten down the line at Old Trafford. He has to push on and play men's football now. He has to improve his physique but he'll work hard to achieve it.'

⊕ Jonny Evans

- ⊕ Position **Centre-back**
- ⊕ Born **2 January 1988, Belfast, Northern Ireland**
- ⊕ Joined United as a trainee **July 2004**

'We have some talented defenders at United – Ferdinand, Brown, Vidic and Pique. Jonny could be one of the very best. He has to be patient and we need to make sure he doesn't develop too soon. Gary Pallister came to United later in his career and I see similarities with Jonny. He's a winner and a good leader, reads the game well and is an all-round good footballer. We have high hopes for him, it's a case of judging when he should play league football.'

THE ART OF GOALSCORING
Ole Gunnar Solskjaer

Ole Gunnar Solskjaer will forever be a part of Old Trafford folklore after his injury-time winner against Bayern Munich sealed United's Treble triumph in 1999. His instinctive strike in Barcelona's Nou Camp stadium was a result of years of honing his goalscoring talents. Here he discusses the five key skills of a top striker...

1 Practice Makes Perfect
'You can't expect to be the best in the world if you don't practise and that extra bit of training can give you the edge. Scoring goals involves two different aspects: shooting and finishing. Shooting is the technique of striking the ball. With finishing, you have to consider other factors such as your position in relation to the goalkeeper and defenders. The more you practise, the more you learn which type of finish is most effective in different positions.'

2 Concentration Is Crucial
'I do lots of fine-tuning in training and repeat the same motion over and over again so I don't have to think about my finishes. Knowing immediately where you want to put the ball means you can concentrate on striking it properly because the art of goalscoring is about how you strike the ball.'

3 Timing Is Everything
'Not only is it important for strikers to time their runs towards the goal, it's crucial to have an understanding of timing with your team-mates. For example, when David Beckham was at United you knew when his crosses were coming and where he would put the ball. The better your understanding with your team-mates, the easier it is to time your run into the right position.'

4 Learn From The Best

'As a youngster I spent hours watching great strikers like Marco van Basten, Kenny Dalglish and Romario. For me, van Basten was the best – his movement and volleying technique were unbelievable. My advice to budding young footballers is if you see something you admire in a game – a goal, a pass or a trick – then go out and practise it yourself.'

5 Believe In Yourself

'Always have the courage to score. Goalscoring is an instinct and is something you're born with; I've always felt that instinct and no matter what positions I've got myself into I've also felt I could score. But you need to possess a certain amount of greed and selfishness to do that. If you believe you can score from any position, you have a great chance of becoming a top striker.'

OLE'S TOP FIVE GOALS

Lille 1-1 United
Stade Félix-Bollaert, Lens, 31 October 2001

'David Beckham's great ball put me in behind the defence. I knew exactly where I wanted to put the ball and fired it towards goal with my left foot. Sometimes you know when you hit a shot that it's going in. I knew with this one even before it flew into the top corner.'

United 2-1 Bayern Munich
Nou Camp, Barcelona, 26 May 1999

'This goal was all about instinct. It's not something you can practise. I was in the right place at the right time and all I focused on was guiding the ball into the net. It was an amazing feeling when it went in. It's a goal I'll never ever forget.'

United 2-2 Chelsea
Old Trafford, 24 September 1997

'Beckham sent a cross-field pass over from the right to where I was stood on the edge of the box. I took one touch to the right and then curled the ball into the far top corner. It was something I'd been practising in training so it was a great feeling to see it fly in.'

United 5-0 Sunderland
Old Trafford, 21 December 1996

'I scored twice in this game but it was my second goal that gave me the most satisfaction because it wasn't one I'd usually score. Having defended a Sunderland free-kick, Peter Schmeichel threw the ball to me in the centre circle. I evaded the last defender and ran from the halfway line before firing it home. I always try to make the keeper move to one side of the goal so it opens up the target. This goal was a good example of that.'

United 2-2 Blackburn
Old Trafford, 25 August 1996

'Aside from the Champions League final goal, I'd say this is my best moment at United. To score on your debut is always a great feeling but the thing I remember most is turning round to see Eric Cantona coming running towards me to celebrate! Another I'll never forget.'

BEHIND THE SCENES
AT SIR ALEX'S WEEKLY
PRESS
CONFERENCE

Friday can be Sir Alex Ferguson's most hectic day of the week. Not only does he finalise preparations for United's weekend game, he also faces the media at his weekly press conference. We tracked the manager's movements as he spoke to the press before United's Premiership clash with Arsenal in April 2006...

10.00 am

Sir Alex assesses his players' fitness ahead of United's upcoming match during an hour's training session.

11.30 am

Journalists and TV crews begin arriving at the state-of-the-art Academy complex at United's Carrington training ground. This is the setting for the manager's pre-match press conference. ManUtd.com, local radio, news agencies and newspaper journalists all attend. Television stations, including MUTV, the club's TV channel, and Sky Sports film the press conference.

12 noon

An immediate hush falls on the room as the United boss arrives and sits down in front of a mass of microphones. First on the agenda is an update on injuries and team news.

11.45 am

At the main Carrington building, Sir Alex meets with the club's Football Media Relations Manager Diana Law who briefs him on any issues in the press that morning.

11.50 am

Sir Alex begins his media activities with a one-on-one interview with MUTV in the training ground's very own television studio. He then makes his way over to the Academy to face the British media.

12.05 pm

For the next 20-25 minutes, Sir Alex fields questions from the gathered reporters on issues ranging from the game with Arsenal to individual players and major issues affecting the club. Reporter: 'What kind of match are you expecting with the Gunners?' Sir Alex: 'We know how to play against Arsenal. Our results have been pleasing against them in our last few meetings. We have some good threats in our team and we will be concentrating on winning the match.'

12.25 pm

The briefing ends and soon the sound of mobile phones and laptops being switched on can be heard as the race to reveal the latest stories from Old Trafford begins. Breaking news is often broadcast on television or announced on ManUtd.com within minutes of the press conference ending.

There can be up to 30 journalists gathering at Carrington for Sir Alex's weekly press briefing. They include...

TV: MUTV, Sky, Granada. Radio: Local radio – Century Radio, Key 103. Press Agencies: Press Association (PA), Reuters. Club Media: ManUtd.com. Daily National Newspapers: Including well-known tabloids the *Sun* and *Daily Mirror*, plus broadsheets such as *The Times* and the *Daily Telegraph*. Local Newspapers: *Manchester Evening News, Oldham Evening Chronicle*. Sunday National Newspapers: Including the *News of the World, Sunday Mirror* and the *Sunday Express*, plus the *Sunday Times* and *Mail on Sunday*.

Giuseppe Rossi

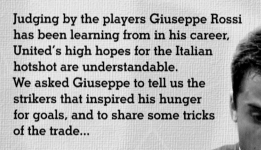

Judging by the players Giuseppe Rossi has been learning from in his career, United's high hopes for the Italian hotshot are understandable. We asked Giuseppe to tell us the strikers that inspired his hunger for goals, and to share some tricks of the trade...

MARCO VAN BASTEN
AC Milan and Holland

The best ever
'I grew up in Italy around the time of the great Milan side in the early 1990s. Marco van Basten is, without doubt, one of the best strikers ever. He had a strong influence on me when I was growing up and first took an interest in football. Technique, finishing, awareness, skill; he had everything, he was complete. Injury ended his career when he was 28 but he scored a ton of goals and was European and World Footballer of the Year on three occasions each.'

All about confidence
The goal he scored for Holland in the 1988 European Championships final was incredible. The ball dropped out of the sky and he volleyed it from the tightest angle straight into the far top corner. It was all about confidence, which came from his ability. You must try things in games even if they're difficult to do. Strikers must always be positive without thinking about missing.'

'ENJOY THE GAME, HAVE FUN AND ALWAYS KEEP YOUR MIND OPEN TO ADVICE'

Q&A

Q: Can you remember your first game?
A: 'Unfortunately, I do. My parents say I didn't move one inch outside the centre circle for the entire match! Luckily I made up for it in my second game – I scored a hat-trick and we won.'

Q: What would be the perfect goal?
A: 'I could say a bicycle kick in the top corner, but a tap-in in a cup final could win your team a trophy. As a striker I love all goals. The ball in the back of the net is all I want to see.'

Q: Does a top striker have to be a natural finisher?
A: 'I think you're born with a gift as a natural goalscorer, especially at the top level. You can work on it and improve, but the likes of van Nistelrooy, Rooney, Solskjaer and Scholes... they have a natural instinct in front of goal.'

Q: Is it important to watch other strikers and learn from them?
A: 'You will always learn from watching football – even just on television. It does you no harm to watch great players.'

Q: What advice would you give to young strikers?
A: 'The most important thing when you are young is to enjoy the game, have fun and always keep your mind open to advice.'

RUUD VAN NISTELROOY
Manchester United and Holland

Best finisher in Europe
'Even before I came to the club I'd seen Ruud score some great goals for United and Holland. He's the best finisher in Europe, just look at his Champions League record. Any striker is judged on goals and Ruud's record speaks for itself. He has this ability to find space in the box, to get away from defenders and be unpredictable with the ball.'

Ruud is ruthless
'Give him a sight of goal and he'll bury his shot. He's ruthless. If Ruud has three chances in a game, he'll bang in two. I learn a lot from him but it's less about him talking to me, and more watching what he does and how he does it.

I try to adapt his qualities to my own game and then put that into a match situation. To have watched him and trained with him is something I feel very fortunate to have experienced.'

ANDREI SHEVCHENKO
Chelsea and Ukraine

He has it all
'Shevchenko has it all. I've been a big fan of his ever since he went to the San Siro from Dynamo Kiev.

As a Milan fan when I was growing up in Italy, he's a player I followed very closely. He's another player that has done it at the highest level. That's what it is all about. He helped Milan win the Champions League final at Old Trafford in 2003 and was named European Footballer of the Year in 2004.

Fantastic technique
'Sheva' has shooting ability, great vision, pace and fantastic technique. He is another complete striker, but he is slightly different to the other two. He uses his pace a lot and sometimes you will find him out wide looking for space, trying to go undetected by defenders. Shevchenko is different to van Basten and van Nistelrooy. But, like I said, it's goals that count and he scores an incredible amount.

Young masters
Gerard Pique

Barcelona-born Gerard Pique wants to combine his cool, calm continental style with some British steel and strength to become a complete defender. We asked him to select three defenders that have helped shape his career, and pass on some top defensive tips...

RONALD KOEMAN
Barcelona and Holland

Koeman was my idol
'One of my earliest memories of football – when I was five – was Ronald Koeman scoring from a free-kick in injury time as Barcelona beat Sampdoria 1-0 in the Champions League final in 1992. I loved watching Koeman play, he was my idol. He wasn't fast, but he was so intelligent and his passing was unbelievable. I enjoy playing the ball out of defence, not just blasting it up to the strikers.'

He was an inspiration
'To be a top defender you can't just make big tackles and clear the ball from danger. You must be a good tackler, position yourself correctly, get your timing right, and be confident enough to control the ball and play it out of defence when necessary. Only the best do that well. Koeman was an inspiration, he played the way I wanted to play.'

RIO FERDINAND
Manchester United and England

Proud to play with Rio
'I'm proud to be at the same club as Rio. Every day in training he helps me a lot and I try to learn from him. All the players talk to me, but Rio especially has given me so much advice. He's been a big help since arriving in Manchester.'

A complete defender
'Rio's passing is fantastic, but he's also a brilliant tackler, with perfect timing and he's strong in the air. Rio is a complete defender. English defenders have a reputation of being big, hard in the tackle and good in the air. Rio is much more than that. That

was a big reason for me coming to Manchester. I looked at Rio and knew the coaches would encourage me to play like that.'

PAOLO MALDINI
AC Milan and Italy

A true great
'I first saw Maldini in 1994 when Barcelona lost 4-0 to Milan in the Champions League final. I've followed him ever since. He's a true great. Maldini has always played at the top, won titles, cups and the Champions League. He's great at left-back and centre-back, and has been captain and loyal to one team. He's a model professional like Ryan Giggs at United. I look up to these players with great admiration.'

An example to all young players
'Maldini is the ultimate defender. His positioning is very clever, he can pass, his timing is first class and he's a brilliant tackler. That's just his football qualities! He's a leader, determined, and loyal... his qualities have no end. Maldini is a rare player and an example to all young players. In football history there have been very few like him.'

'DON'T THINK "I MUST DO IT WELL" AND PRESSURE YOURSELF. YOUR BEST PERFORMANCES COME WHEN YOU'RE RELAXED.'

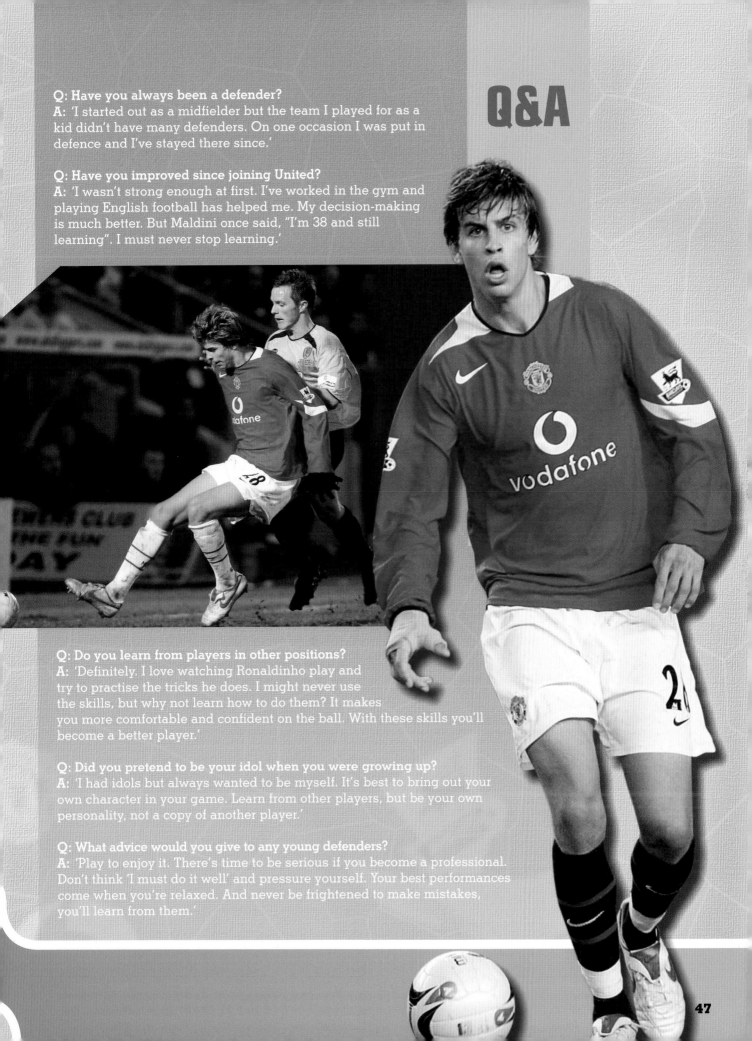

Q: Have you always been a defender?
A: 'I started out as a midfielder but the team I played for as a kid didn't have many defenders. On one occasion I was put in defence and I've stayed there since.'

Q: Have you improved since joining United?
A: 'I wasn't strong enough at first. I've worked in the gym and playing English football has helped me. My decision-making is much better. But Maldini once said, "I'm 38 and still learning". I must never stop learning.'

Q: Do you learn from players in other positions?
A: 'Definitely. I love watching Ronaldinho play and try to practise the tricks he does. I might never use the skills, but why not learn how to do them? It makes you more comfortable and confident on the ball. With these skills you'll become a better player.'

Q: Did you pretend to be your idol when you were growing up?
A: 'I had idols but always wanted to be myself. It's best to bring out your own character in your game. Learn from other players, but be your own personality, not a copy of another player.'

Q: What advice would you give to any young defenders?
A: 'Play to enjoy it. There's time to be serious if you become a professional. Don't think 'I must do it well' and pressure yourself. Your best performances come when you're relaxed. And never be frightened to make mistakes, you'll learn from them.'

Who's who
ON THE BENCH?

IT'S NOT ONLY SIR ALEX FERGUSON
AND THE SUBSTITUTES THAT OCCUPY
THE DUG-OUT ON MATCHDAYS.
ALONGSIDE THEM ARE ESSENTIAL
BACKROOM STAFF WHO ALL HAVE
VITAL ROLES AT THE CLUB. THIS
IS A GUIDED TOUR OF THE HOME
DUG-OUT AT OLD TRAFFORD.

1 **SIR ALEX FERGUSON MANAGER**
Season joined 1986/87
This is the manager's regular spot in the Old Trafford
dug-out. He rarely sits down during home matches,
and often makes his way to the touchline to give
instructions to his players.

2 **ROB SWIRE HEAD PHYSIO**
Season joined 1991/92
You'll see Rob running onto the pitch to treat United's
injured players during matches. He also helps
prevent injuries, working closely with the medical
staff to ensure players warm up and warm down
from games properly.

3 **ALBERT MORGAN KIT MANAGER**
Season joined 1993/94
Matchdays are extremely busy for Albert, who
ensures each player has the correct kit – including
warm-up and match gear. He also prepares three
pairs of boots for each player for every game.

4 **VALTER DI SALVO FITNESS COACH**
Season joined 2004/05
The former Lazio and Real Madrid fitness coach
assists Carlos Queiroz and Mike Phelan during
training and co-ordinates the team's pre-match
warm-up. He has also developed individual fitness
programmes for all the players.

5 **DARREN FLETCHER FIRST TEAM PLAYER**

6 **PHIL BARDSLEY FIRST TEAM PLAYER**

7 **CARLOS QUEIROZ FIRST TEAM ASSISTANT MANAGER**
Season joined 2002/03 Rejoined 2004/05
The former Real Madrid manager takes charge
of training at Carrington on a daily basis. On
matchdays he is often seen instructing players from
the touchline or talking tactics with Sir Alex.

⑧ MIKE PHELAN FIRST TEAM COACH
Season joined 1999/2000

The former United midfielder works alongside Carlos and Valter in preparing the players for games. He always has a pen and paper close at hand to take tactical notes throughout the match.

⑨ ALEC WYLIE ASSISTANT KIT MANAGER
Season joined 1984/85

Alec is one of the backroom staff's longest-serving members. He assists Albert ensuring the kit is ready for every first-team match, both at home and abroad. He also looks after the Reserves' kit.

⑩ GARRY ARMER MASSEUR
Season joined 2002/03

Garry is one of two masseurs at the club alongside Rod Thornley. He focuses on the conditioning of the players' bodies before and after matches, getting rid of muscular aches and pains.

⑪ TONY COTON GOALKEEPING COACH
Season joined 1998/99

A former United keeper, 'TC' works with the first-team goalkeepers and the club's young stoppers. On matchdays he puts Edwin van der Sar and co. through their paces during the pre-match warm-up.

THE CHANGING FACE OF
OLD TRAFFORD

Following Old Trafford's expansion to a capacity of over 76,000, it remains one of the finest and most well-known football stadiums in the world. Here are some little known facts about the recent development of the Theatre of Dreams...

FACTS AND FIGURES

- Building work on the north-west and north-east quadrants began at the end of the 2004/05 season.

- The project took 62 weeks to complete.

- The north-west quadrant was finished slightly before its north-east neighbour.

- There is an added 2,949 square metres of hospitality, conference and event space, increasing the number of matchday diners by almost 45 per cent.

- Around 600,000 man-hours were spent on the expansion process, with up to 450 workers on site at any one time.

- The project used up over 4,000 cubic metres of concrete, around 3,500 tonnes of steel and a combined total of 1,366 pre-cast units were pieced together to form the new terracing.

- The roofing above the quadrants covers approximately 4,900 square metres and about 9,000 square metres of new walls have been erected.

- United set a new Premiership attendance record against Birmingham in March 2006 when the first seats in the north-west quadrant were made available, with 69,070 fans at the game.

- Old Trafford's record attendance of 70,504 (against Aston Villa on 27 December 1920) was finally broken during the 2-0 win over Arsenal in April 2006 when the capacity reached 70,908. During the 2006/07 season it will pass the 76,000 mark.

> 'IT'S GREAT TO PLAY IN FRONT OF SO MANY PEOPLE – IT'S A STAGE ANY PLAYER WANTS TO BE ON. IT WAS ALREADY A MAGNIFICENT STADIUM, NOW IT'S EVEN BETTER.'
> DARREN FLETCHER

> 'THE EXPANSION SHOWS THE PROGRESS THE CLUB IS MAKING. WE HAVE TO TRY AND BE THE BEST AND, IF POSSIBLE, WE SHOULD MAKE THIS STADIUM AS BIG AS WE CAN.'
> SIR ALEX FERGUSON

Gary Neville and former players Alex Stepney (left) and
Denis Irwin (right) announce the naming of the 500 Club.

'PLAYING IN FRONT OF OVER 76,000
FANS IS SOMETHING VERY SPECIAL.
I DON'T THINK THERE'S A BETTER
FOOTBALL STADIUM IN THE WORLD.'
GARY NEVILLE

STADIUM FACILITIES

Brand new Executive Suites have also
been created. They include...

- **THE 100 CLUB**
  **Pays tribute to the players who have scored
  more than 100 goals for United**
- **THE 500 CLUB**
  **Represents the elite group to make over
  500 appearances**

The north-east quadrant, part of the expansion of Old Trafford,
which took the stadium capacity to over 76,000.

The new Sports Bar in the 500 Club which is situated in the
north-east quadrant.

- **THE ACADEMY AND THE KIT ROOM**
- **THE CAPTAINS' LOUNGE**
  Honours United's greatest skippers
- **THE KNIGHTS' LOUNGE**
  **Celebrates the success of United's three Sirs –
  Matt Busby, Bobby Charlton and Alex Ferguson**
- **THE 1968 AND 1999 SUITES**
  Reflect on the club's two European Cup triumphs
- **THE GALLERY**
- **EVOLUTION**
  Celebrates the life of the Theatre of Dreams
- **SUPER SUITES**
- **EXECUTIVE BOXES**

51

1000
PREMIERSHIP GOALS

United reached the landmark goals total on 29 October 2005. Unfortunately, when Cristiano Ronaldo's injury-time header flew in, it was only a consolation in a 4-1 defeat at Middlesbrough. But there are plenty of great goals to look back on, and we've picked three of the Reds' most memorable Premiership net-busters...

STEVE BRUCE – GOAL NO. 54
United 2-1 Sheffield Wednesday
Old Trafford, 10 April 1993

Having already headed a crucial equaliser with just four minutes of normal time remaining, Steve Bruce headed in a second after Gary Pallister's deflected cross. Deep into injury time, it kept United on course for their first Premiership title. Cue wild celebrations from a jubilant Sir Alex Ferguson and his assistant Brian Kidd, who danced with delight on the Old Trafford turf.

DAVID BECKHAM – GOAL NO. 300
Wimbledon 0-3 United
Selhurst Park, 17 August 1996

One of the most audacious goals ever scored. And to think Becks was just 21 when he fired home this strike from the halfway line. With United already leading 2-0 in their opening game of the 1996/97 season, the midfielder saw Dons keeper Neil Sullivan off his line and tried his luck. The end product was phenomenal.

FACTS AND FIGURES

- 27 of United's 1,000 goals came courtesy of opposition own goals.

- Southampton have taken the brunt of United's goalscoring firepower, shipping 61 goals in 26 games against the Reds.

- Arch-rivals Liverpool were seventh in the list, conceding 40 times in 27 games. Arsenal found themselves in 14th place after seeing United fire 35 goals past them in 26 games, while Chelsea followed soon after in 16th, having conceded 34 goals in 26 matches.

- Andy Cole (93 goals from 195 appearances), Ryan Giggs (87 in 411 games) and Paul Scholes (87 in 331 matches) were the Reds' top three Premiership marksmen in the first 1,000 goals.

- United's favourite away ground during the march to their millennium milestone was Everton's Goodison Park where they scored 28 goals. Selhurst Park (24) and St. James' Park (23) were next in the list of fruitful road trips.

ANDY COLE – GOAL NO. 526
United 2-1 Tottenham Hotspur
Old Trafford, 16 May 1999

With the score level at 1-1 in United's final must-win match of the season, substitute Andy Cole was introduced at half-time and took just two minutes to make his mark. His controlled looping effort over Spurs keeper Ian Walker helped United reclaim the Premiership title from Arsenal's grasp and set the Reds on their way to an incredible Treble.

1000 GOALS

Here is a season-by-season guide to United's 1,000 Premiership goals...

1992/93	**67 goals**
1993/94	**80 goals**
1994/95	**77 goals**
1995/96	**73 goals**
1996/97	**76 goals**
1997/98	**73 goals**
1998/99	**80 goals**
1999/00	**97 goals**
2000/01	**79 goals**
2001/02	**87 goals**
2002/03	**74 goals**
2003/04	**64 goals**
2004/05	**58 goals**
2005/06	**15 goals**

(up to and including United's 1000th goal)

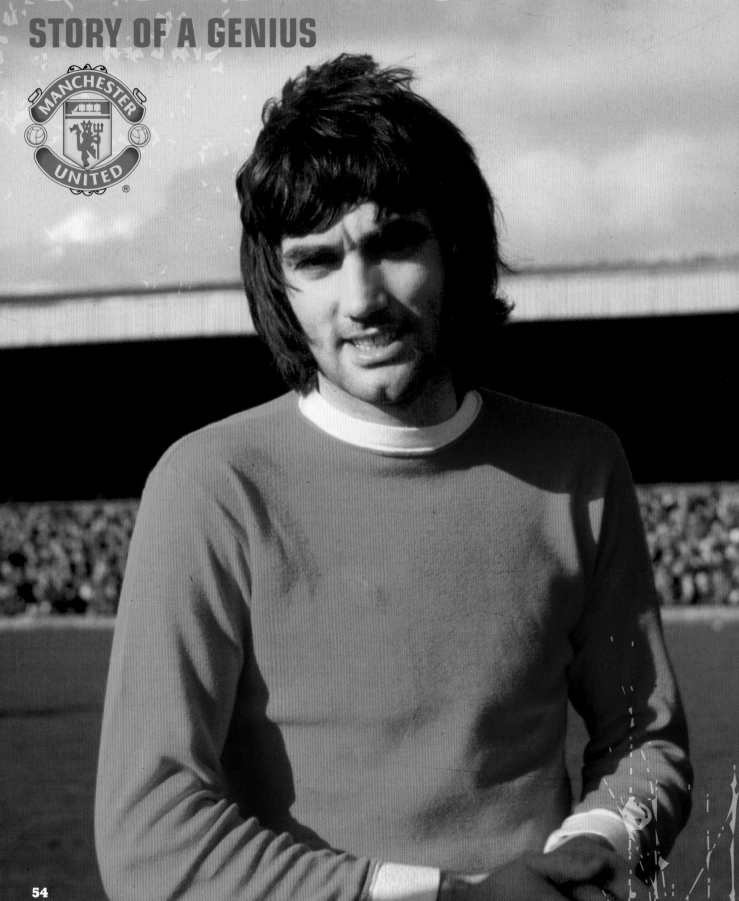

GEORGE BEST

STORY OF A GENIUS

GEORGE BEST'S DEATH IN NOVEMBER 2005 LEFT MANCHESTER UNITED AND FOOTBALL FANS WORLDWIDE MOURNING THE LOSS OF A GENIUS. ONE THING IS FOR CERTAIN, HOWEVER, THIS LEGEND WILL NEVER BE FORGOTTEN...

In 1961, United scout Bob Bishop sent a telegram to former United manager Matt Busby. It read, 'I've found you a genius.' He had just watched a skinny 15-year-old lad playing for his local team Cregagh Boys Club in Northern Ireland. His name: George Best. He signed for the Reds shortly after and made his United debut at Old Trafford against West Bromwich Albion in September 1963, aged 17. Best combined the courage of Wayne Rooney, the speed of a young Ryan Giggs and the jinking runs of Cristiano Ronaldo. United's supporters idolised him almost immediately. He helped the Reds win league titles in 1965 and 1967, before reaching the peak of his powers in 1968 when United won the European Cup and Best was named European Footballer of the Year and Football Writers' Player of the Year. He scored 28 goals that season, dazzling fans and terrorising defenders with his skill. He scored 178 goals in 466 appearances for the Reds between 1963 and 1974 – an incredible record for a winger. To many, George Best was the best.

KEY MOMENTS

- George Best was born in Belfast on 22 May 1946
- United scout Bob Bishop spotted him playing for Cregagh Boys Club in 1961, aged 15
- He made his United debut in a 1-0 home win against West Brom on 14 September 1963
- In 1968, he became the youngest-ever European Footballer of the Year at the age of 21
- In the same year he helped United win the European Cup, scoring a crucial goal in the 4-1 win over Benfica
- He found the net six times in United's 8-2 FA Cup win over Northampton Town in 1970
- Despite leaving Old Trafford aged 26, Best played 466 games for the Reds, scoring 178 goals

HONOURS

Football League Championship 1965, 1967
European Cup 1968
European Footballer of the Year 1968
Football Writers' Player of the Year 1968
English Football Hall of Fame 2002
PFA Special Merit Award 2006

George Best watches from the directors' box during the Premiership match between Portsmouth and Manchester United at Fratton Park on 30 October 2004.

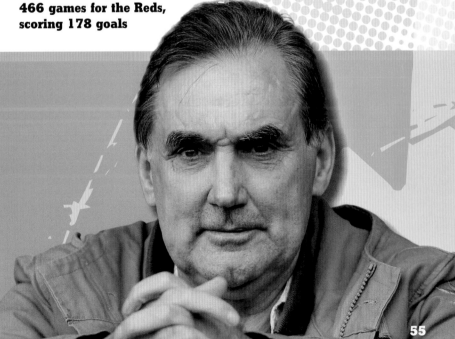

IN THE WORDS OF OTHERS...

'George produced breathtaking performances, single-handedly winning matches. He was incredibly talented and gifted.'
Sir Alex Ferguson

'This club's glorious history was created by people like George Best. Anyone that witnessed what he could do on the pitch wished they could do the same.'
Sir Bobby Charlton

'Best was one of the greatest footballers ever, if not the greatest.'
Wayne Rooney

'He could use either foot – sometimes he seemed to have six.'
Sir Matt Busby

'I'd love George to save me a place in his team in heaven.'
Eric Cantona

'The closest I got to him was when we shook hands at the end of the game.'
Northampton Town player Roy Fairfax after Best scored six goals in United's 8-2 FA Cup win in 1970

Red Dates
For Your Diary

Need to know the date Manchester United was born, or when Sir Matt Busby won his first trophy at Old Trafford? These are the essential dates every United diary should include...

1878
The club is formed as Newton Heath Lancashire and Yorkshire Railway Football Club by railworkers in Newton Heath, Manchester.

20 NOVEMBER 1880
Newton Heath plays its first recorded match, a 0-6 defeat away at Bolton Wanderers.

28 APRIL 1902
Manchester United FC is born. The club also announces its intention to change the colours from Newton Heath's green and yellow to red.

11 MARCH 1941
During the Second World War, the German air force, the Luftwaffe, pay Old Trafford a visit and cause substantial damage to the stadium. United are forced to play their games at City's Maine Road ground until 1949.

19 FEBRUARY 1945
Matt Busby agrees to become United manager.

24 April 1948
The Reds claim their first piece of silverware under Matt Busby's leadership with a 4-2 win against Blackpool in the FA Cup final at Wembley.

6 JUNE 1953
Bobby Charlton arrives at Old Trafford, four months after being spotted by United scout Joe Armstrong.

6 FEBRUARY 1958
Tragedy strikes when the plane carrying the team back from Belgrade crashes during take-off at Munich Airport at 3.04 pm, killing 23 people on board including eight players.

16 AUGUST 1961
United sign a young apprentice by the name of George Best.

18 AUGUST 1962
Denis Law scores on his Reds debut during a 2-2 draw with West Brom at Old Trafford.

29 MAY 1968
United become the first English club to win the European Cup following a 4-1 win over Benfica at Wembley.

3 OCTOBER 1981
Bryan Robson joins United for £1.5million and signs his contract on the pitch before the home game with Wolves.

6 NOVEMBER 1986
Alex Ferguson is named as United manager.

7 JANUARY 1990
Mark Robins' winning goal at Nottingham Forest in the FA Cup third round sets up Alex Ferguson on the way to his first trophy with the club.

19 DECEMBER 1992
Eric Cantona scores the first of his 82 goals for the Reds during the 1-1 Premiership draw at Chelsea.

2 MAY 1993
Alex Ferguson becomes the first manager to win the title on both sides of the border after Aston Villa's 1-0 defeat to Oldham Athletic hands United the Championship. He also led Aberdeen to the title in Scotland.

19 JULY 1993
Alex Ferguson secures the services of Nottingham Forest midfielder Roy Keane in a then record £3.75million deal.

26 MAY 1999
The Treble! Ole Gunnar Solskjaer and Teddy Sheringham complete United's triple glory in Barcelona's Nou Camp.

28 SEPTEMBER 2004
Wayne Rooney hits a hat-trick in his first match in a red shirt as United crush Champions League opponents Fenerbahce 6-2.

THE GREAT UNITED QUIZ

Are you United's most knowledgeable supporter? Can you remember when Ole Solskjaer arrived at Old Trafford and how many goals Gabriel Heinze scored on his United debut? Test yourself with two pages of fun quizzes and competitions...

TRUE OR FALSE?

1. Wayne Rooney joined United on the final day of the 2004 transfer window.

2. Ryan Giggs once played for England schoolboys even though he is Welsh.
3. Rio Ferdinand scored for England during the 1998 World Cup in France.
4. Paul Scholes is an Oldham Athletic fan.
5. Gabriel Heinze scored twice on his United debut.

GOALMOUTH SCRAMBLE

Unscramble the letters below to reveal the surnames of ten current United players...

LLEINVE   ZNEHIE   **NWBOR**   NOYEOR
LSEHCSO   **HREFTCLE**   HMIST   GGSIG
DOLANRO   CIDVI

IN THIS YEAR...

Name the year in which all of the following happened at Old Trafford:

1. Eric Cantona was named the Football Writers' Player of the Year.
2. United won the League and Cup double for a second time under Sir Alex Ferguson.
3. Ole Gunnar Solskjaer joined the Reds.
4. Steve Bruce left United on a free transfer to join Birmingham.

WHO AM I?

Match the following descriptions to the correct current players...

1. A former student at the FA School of Excellence at Lilleshall, this Longsight-born defender made his first team debut in May 1998. Sir Alex Ferguson has since described him as 'the best natural defender this club has had for years.'
2. This player cost just over £12million when United bought him in August 2003, a week after playing against him in a pre-season friendly with Sporting Lisbon. He was named the Sir Matt Busby Player of the Year at the end of his first season at Old Trafford.

3. One of United's longest serving players and a Red through and through. He joined the club as a trainee in July 1991 and was handed the captain's armband following the departure of Roy Keane midway through the 2005/06 campaign.
4. This American-born Italian striker joined United's Academy from Serie A outfit Parma in July 2004. A natural goalscorer, he marked his senior Premiership debut with a goal just nine minutes after coming on as a sub.

3

4

Quick Quiz

SPOT THE BALL

Wayne Rooney is always closely marked by opposing defenders. Arsenal right-back Lauren was tight to his man when the two teams met at Highbury in January 2006. We've removed the ball from the picture, your challenge is to pick the grid square the ball is in.

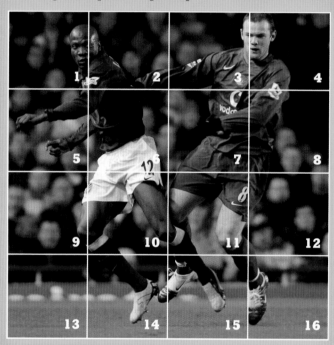

SCORE A ROONEY HAT-TRICK

1. How many goals did Wayne Rooney score in 2005/06?
2. Against which team did Rooney make his United debut?
3. United beat Arsenal 2-0 at Old Trafford in April 2006. Rooney scored first, who got the second goal?

GUESS WHO?

United's players are unmistakable on the pitch, but can you identify the players being put through their paces in training?

1. Louis Saha and Rio Ferdinand laugh during training, but who is their Reds team-mate?
2. Is it cold or has this young Reds star hit a shot wide in training? Do you know who it is?

3. An early morning training session for this United player, but which Reds star is it?
4. Nemanja Vidic is on his trail, but who is the Reds midfielder in the hat?

Fixtures 2006/07

AUGUST 2006

Sun 20	Fulham	(H)	1.30pm
Wed 23	Charlton Athletic	(A)	8.00pm
Sat 26	Watford	(A)	

SEPTEMBER 2006

Sat 9	Tottenham Hotspur	(H)	5.15pm
Sun 17	Arsenal	(H)	4.00pm
Sat 23	Reading	(A)	5.15pm
Sat 30	Newcastle United	(H)	

OCTOBER 2006

Sat 14	Wigan Athletic	(A)	12.45pm
Sun 22	Liverpool	(H)	1.00pm
Wed 25	Carling Cup 3rd Rd		
Sat 28	Bolton Wanderers	(A)	

NOVEMBER 2006

Sat 4	Portsmouth	(H)	
Wed 8	Carling Cup 4th Rd		
Sat 11	Blackburn Rovers	(A)	5.15pm
Sat 18	Sheffield United	(A)	
Sun 26	Chelsea	(H)	4.00pm
Wed 29	Everton	(H)	

DECEMBER 2006

Sat 2	Middlesbrough	(A)	5.15pm
Sat 9	Manchester City	(H)	12.45pm
Sun 17	West Ham United	(A)	4.00pm
Wed 20	Carling Cup 5th Rd		
Sat 23	Aston Villa	(A)	
Tue 26	Wigan Athletic	(H)	
Sat 30	Reading	(H)	

JANUARY 2007

Mon 1	Newcastle United	(A)	
Sat 6	FA Cup 3rd Rd		
Wed 10	Carling Cup Semi-final (1st leg)		
Sat 13	Aston Villa	(H)	
Sat 20	Arsenal	(A)	
Wed 24	Carling Cup Semi-final (2nd leg)		
Sat 27	FA Cup 4th Rd		
Wed 31	Watford	(H)	

FEBRUARY 2007

Sat 3	Tottenham Hotspur	(A)	
Sat 10	Charlton Athletic	(H)	
Sat 17	FA Cup 5th Rd		
Sat 24	Fulham	(A)	
Sun 25	Carling Cup Final		

MARCH 2007

Sat 3	Liverpool	(A)	
Sat 10	FA Cup 6th Rd		
Sat 17	Bolton Wanderers	(H)	
Sat 31	Blackburn Rovers	(H)	

APRIL 2007

Sat 7	Portsmouth	(A)	
Tue 10	Sheffield United	(H)	
Sat 14	Chelsea/ FA Cup Semi-final	(A)	
Sat 21	Middlesbrough	(H)	
Sat 28	Everton	(A)	12.00noon

MAY 2007

Sat 5	Manchester City	(A)	
Sun 13	West Ham United	(H)	3.00pm
Sat 19	FA Cup Final*